CEMETERY
RECORDS
of
Martic Township
Lancaster County
Pennsylvania

Jenne Renkin

HERITAGE BOOKS
2007

HERITAGE BOOKS

AN IMPRINT OF HERITAGE BOOKS, INC.

Books, CDs, and more—Worldwide

For our listing of thousands of titles see our website
at
www.HeritageBooks.com

Published 2007 by
HERITAGE BOOKS, INC.
Publishing Division
65 East Main Street
Westminster, Maryland 21157-5026

International Standard Book Number: 978-1-58549-448-4

CONTENTS

INTRODUCTION

The following data was taken from inscriptions of tombstones of every existing church cemetery in Martic Township. In addition we have included Clearfield M.E. Church Cemetery in Providence Township and Colemanville Methodist Church Cemetery in Conestoga Township. Both are located near the Martic Township border. I copied most of the tombstones within the past twenty-five years with additional data added within the past year (1996-7). An appendix has been added which summarizes the known veterans buried in Martic Township.

Martic Township was established in 1729 with the formation of Lancaster County. The early settlers of Martic Township were principally Scots-Irish and thus a large portion of the population was Presbyterian. By the 1830s Methodists outnumbered the Presbyterians. Today the Presbyterian churches have disappeared leaving three Methodist churches and a single Mennonite church. The Rawlinsville Mennonite Church was formed in 1929. For more details on the records of the churches and cemeteries of Lancaster County, see A. Hunter Rineer, Jr., *Churches And Cemeteries Of Lancaster County, Pennsylvania. A Complete Guide*, published by the Lancaster County Historical Society, 1993.

The following abbreviations were used:

b. - born	Inf. - Infantry
Co. - Company	m - months
d - days	m. - mother
d. - died	m/o - mother of
dau. - daughter	Reg. - Regiment
d/o - daughter of	s/o - son of
f. - father	w - weeks
GAR - Grand Army of the Republic	w. - wife
	w/o - wife of
gch. - grandchildren	y - years

Jenne Renkin
Lancaster, Pennsylvania
1997

MARTIC TOWNSHIP CEMETERIES

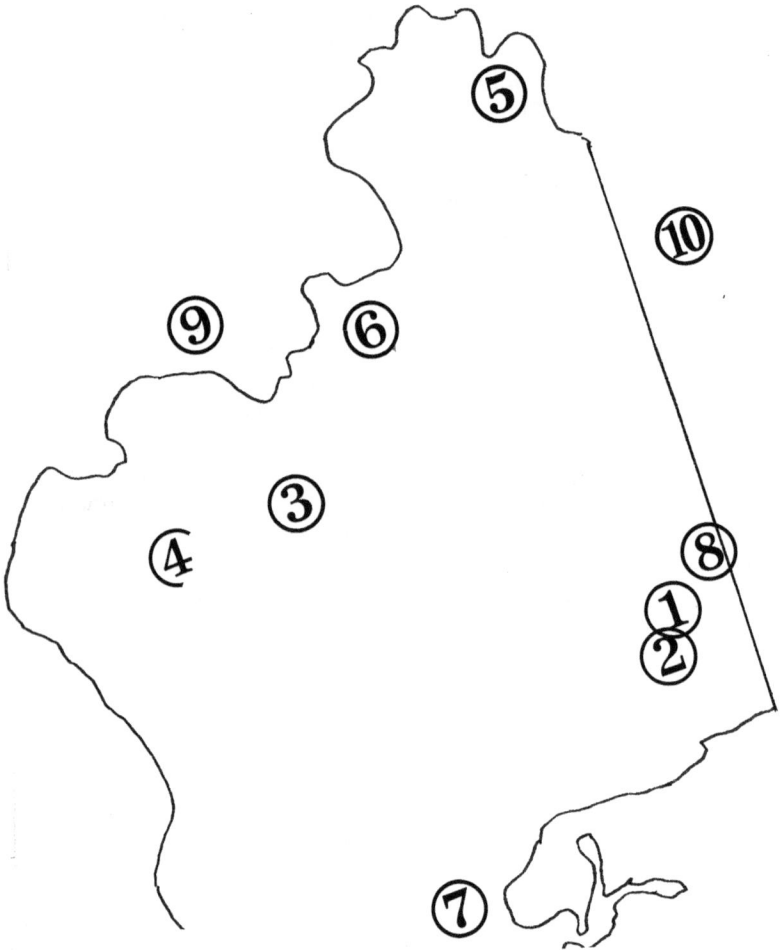

1. Muddy Run Presbyterian Cemetery, Rawlinsville
2. Rawlinsville Mennonite Church Cemetery
3. Mount Nebo Methodist Church Cemetery
4. Mt. Nebo Presbyterian Church Cemetery (Also Clark's Cemetery)
5. Marticville Methodist Cemetery
6. Flory Mill Cemetery
7. Bethesda Methodist Church Cemetery
8. Rawlinsville Methodist Church Cemetery
9. Colemanville Methodist Church Cemetery
10. Clearfield M. E. Church Cemetery

MUDDY RUN PRESBYTERIAN CEMETERY, RAWLINSVILLE

Compiled by Jenne Renkin and Mrs. Claire Frantz on 25 Aug. 1971.
Recopied by Jenne Renkin in December 1978.

The church was built of log in 1742. A one-story stone church was built
in 1853 and torn down in 1978. The cemetery was behind the church
which is now gone.

Row 1
Dunkle, James, No dates

Row 2
Cramer, Martha, 10/6/1833-11/25/1912, 89y
Cramer, Benjamin, 1/7/1828-5/27/1902, 74y
Cramer, Nancy, d. 5/2/1835, 82 y
Cramer, Harriet, 12/22/1829-10/25/1905
C.K./M.A.K.
Krieder, Calvin, s/o John & Eliz., 7/30/1867-11/2/1890, 23y
Krieder, Francis J., 1864-1900
Krieder, Anna E., his wife, 1868-1941
Krieder, Martha A., w/o Martin Krider, 9/10/1848-7/27/1885, 36y
8 children, tombstone, unnamed
Krieder, Benjamin, b. & d. 6/22/1866
Krieder, Elizabeth, 84y
Kreider, John, 3/20/1834-
Kreider, Unetta, 1872- 17

Row 3
Cramer, Mary, d. 9/_/1887
Cramer, Anna, 1870-1871
Cramer, Elce, d. 1886
Cramer, Harrison, d. 1888
Cramer, Robert, d. 8/24/1890
Cramer, George, d. 5/31/1903, 21y
Cramer, Daniel, Co. K, 79th Pa. Vol., father, 9/24/1843-8/13/1935
Cramer, Sarah, mother, 2/23/1848-3/27/1910
Simpson, James, d. 11/19/1885, 85y
Simpson, Jane, d. 2/8/1888, 75y
Simpson, Mary, d. 5/15/1890, 91y
Simpson, Sarah, d. 1/21/1829, 81y
Simpson, Bartholomew, 10/15/1818-3/9/1901, 82y
Miller, David, d. 3/26/1898, 78 y
Miller, Mary, 6/23/1826-1/23/1904

Row 4
Douts, Mary, d. 7/10/1880, 87y
Douts, William, d. 1/16/1873, 92y
Culy, Thomas, 6/22/1812-10/20/1865
Davidson, Alice, 8/11/1806-11/21/1863
Doulin, Mary Jane, 2/3/1850-11/8/1864
Savery, William T., d. 9/15/1835-1861

Row 5
Smith, Harriet Ann Steveson, 1836-1919
Steveson, Elizabeth Jane, 1851-1930
Steveson, Elizabeth, 8/12/1809-11/07/1855, 46y
Steveson, John, 1807-1896, 88y
____ [cannot read stone]
Simpson, Wallace, d. 1832, 3y
Wallace, Nancy, w/o John, d. 4/13/1837, 70y
Wallace, John, d. 6/30/1855
Wallace, Matha, w/o William, d. 3/11/1856, 6y
Wallace, ___ [broken stone, cannot read]
Wallace, Nancy, 3/22/1822-8/5/1895
Wallace, Sarah, 11/_/1829-5/_/1900
Wallace, Mary A., 1/_/1825-4/_/1918
Wallace, Elenora E., 9/_/1831-1/_/1913?
Savery, George S., 9/10/1785-2/_/1849, 65y
Savery, Ann, age 14mos.; Edward, age 14mos.; ch/J...S. & M.L.

Row 6
VanDyke, Elizabeth, w/o Joseph, 12/4/1820-11/30/1894
M. small broken stone
Creamer, Peter, d. 10/11/1836, 83y
Creamer, Mary, w/o Peter, d.d 1/12/1843, 81y5m3d
Overholizer, Ann, w/o Daniel (d/o B. & E. Good), 12/31/1831-8/4/1850,
    18y7m3d
Good, B., no dates
Good, E., no dates
Burns, Robert, brother, 9/1/1835-7/31/1900
Me-Deth [3rd letter missing], Charles, d. 7/7/1833
Row 7
Miller, Elizabeth, 11/10/1825-7/16/1905
Miller, John, 4/21/1791-4/28/1865, 71y7d
Miller, Samuel, d. 4/11/1865, 50y10m8d
Miller, Elizabeth, w/o John, 1/23/1792-4/27/1858, 66y3m1d
Miller, Benjamin, s/o J. & E., 2/8/1816-8/10/1844, 28y6m2d
Miller, P.M.
Miller, James P., s/o J. & E., 7/22/1831-10/2/1854, 23y

Miller, Sarah, d/o J. & E., 2/26/1828-10/26/1878
Miller, Mary, d/o J. & E., 10/19/1823-10/29/1851
Miller, Joseph P., d. 11/25/1901,70y3m24d
Burns, William, father, 2/12/1808-12/10/1870, 71y3m24d
Burns, Rebecca, w/o William, mother, 2/4/1809-12/23/1891, 82y10m19d
Burns, C.
Burns, W.
Burns, Elizabeth, 7/11/1845-2/15/1866, 19y1m4d
Burns, Harriet C., sister, d/o W. & R., 8/4/1833-1/1/1902, 58y4m27d
Burns, Daniel, GAR, 3/23/1838-12/3/1906, 65y8m9d
Burns, Hettie, w/o Daniel, 10/7/1853-10/19/1887, 34y4m12d
Burns, infant children of Daniel & Hettie, no dates
Frazer, Margaret, w/o David, d/o James Brown, d. 10/7/1827, 28y

Row 8
Duncan, James, most of stone buried, d. 9/10/1765

Row 9
Gray, Hugh, cut in slate marker, d. 1/25/1760, 51y
Duncan, William, cut in slate marker, d. 9/13/1744
Rennel, Sarah, cut in slate marker, d. 2/15/1750, 52y
Pegan, James, 7/25/1796-4/11/1875, 78y8m12d
Pegan, Isaac A., s/o James & Janet, d. 8/12/1846d, 12y8d
Gainer, Mary, w/o Alexander Gainer, d. 6/11/1848, 71y

Row 10
Leman, William Jun., d. 11/16/1760, 22y
Leman, William Sr., d. 3/4/1772, 80y
Leman, George, d. 1/12/1791, 52y
Leman, Ann Hill, d. 10/30/1822, 73y
"Here lie the bodies of Wm. Leman and his two sons and his son's wife,
     Ann Hill, in one grave to moulder in the clay with each other."
Lemon, William, 4/29/1773-8/20/1847, 74y3m22d
Lemon, Martha, w/o Wm. Leman, d. 3/11/1857, 86y10m17d
___, rough field stone

Row 11
Simpson, Jane, w/o John, d. 1/4/1858, 80y
Simpson, John Sr., b. Scotland, 11/16/1770-5/16/1852, 81y6m
Simpson, John Jr., 7/17/1816-4/13/1835, 18y11m26d
Simpson, Alice S. d/o J. & J.S., 1/18/1807-11/28/1808, 1y10m

Row 12
Conway, John, Co. H. 203d Pa. Ind. GAR, no dates
A.D., small stone, no dates, leaning on fence.

MARTICVILLE METHODIST CEMETERY

Copied from *The Receding Shadows of Time*, by Larry E. Hess.
With additional data by Jenne Renkin, Dec. 1978

Row 1
Hart, Albertus, 1855-1934
Hart, Hannah J., 1859-1933
Shultz, Katherine E., 1879-1955
Shultz, Ezra H., 12/25/1873-12/28/1937. Father
Jones, Dorothy Jane, d/o Rev. RH & PF, 1931-1931
Wilson, Mary, w/o Mathias, 5/22/1816-11/19/1894, 78y5m27d
Wilson, Matthias, 2/18/1811-2/26/1901, 90y8m
Warfel, Elizabath, d. March 1902, 75y
Warfel, Elias, d. 3/_/1902, 83y
McGaw, Richard C., son, 1917-1933
McGaw, Minnie B. his w., 1884-1962
McGaw, James W., 1870-1949
Stripe, Nellie F., m., 1901-1957
Kleinhans, Alice S. Helm, wife, 1883-1965
Kleinhans, Elias L., 1847-1910

Row 2
Mundorf, Bertha L., 7/31/1888-3/21/1953. Mother
Mundorf, Howard M., 2/14/1882-5/21/1934. Father
Henry, Norman R. (Wallis E. 1900-71, Martha Hess 1897- [his parents]),
    1923-1924

Row 3
Bleacher, Martin, Co. H 79 Reg. Pa. Vol., 7/21/1841-7/10/1904, 62y11m19d
Bleacher, Eliza, 12/29/1851-12/27/1913, 61y11m29d
Bleacher, Ferdie, s/o of, 2/20/1876-9/2/1888
Worfel, Susan B., his w., 1850-1942
Worfel, Daniel H., 1847-1935
Shultz, Harry, 1850-1927
Shultz, Sara J., his w., 1851-1940
Shultz, Millard F., 1875-1948
Myers, Susan D., 1869-1930. Mother
Myers, George W., 1867-1924. Father
Myers, Mattias, 8/18/1824-9/22/1914, 90y
Myers, Martha, 3/3/1829-7/26/1873
Myers, Ida M., d/o Matthias & Martha, d. 6/14/1904
Shoff, Howard, s/o Abraham & Emily, 3/18/1839-3/22/1841
Shoff, Harry M., s/o Abraham & Emily, 6/22/1889-8/24/1889
Shoff, Ida M., d/o Abraham & Emily, 3/26/1881-8/31/1887

Elmire, Irene M., 1865-1959
Whirlow, Harry, 1865-1962

Rows 4 and 5
Alexander, Charles E., 1897-
Alexander, Blanche V., 1900-
Klein, Hans Elias, 1847-1910. Klein, Annie M., his wife, 1852-1939
Eshleman, David R., 9/17/1894-12/30/1971
Eshleman, Lillie R., 3/25/1899-
Appel, Elwood S., 1932-
Appel, Charlotte R., 1938-
Kilmer, Rexford P., 8/18/1907-

MARTICVILLE METHODIST CHURCH & CEMETERY

ELLIS & EVANS, *History of Lancaster County, Pennsylvania*, 1883, pg. 975 noted that: "The oldest cemetery in this township is attached to the Methodist Episcopal Church at Marticville." The first interment antedates the French & Indian War. It was used by miners of the Pequea Silver Mines, in Pequea Twp. The oldest burial noted in this project was in Row 22 - GOOD, PETER d. 1746, Margt. d. 1762.

The congregation was organized in 1836. Meetings were held in homes until 1863 when they met at Huber's Hall. Later a stone church was built in 1874. Land was obtained from Eli Eshleman by Trustees, Henry Brooks, Samuel Bookman, Matthias Myers, Henry Charles, Abraham Charles & John D. Sensenig. In 1883 the trustees were the following persons: Henry Brooks, David S. McElhaney, Gabriel Spence, David Fehl, Jas. Creamer. Ministers: 1874-1883 Rev. John Herr, Fredr. Brady, John W. Harkins, J. A. Amber. This church was part of the Safe Harbor Circuit.

This church is 11.1 miles from Lancaster City, Penna. Proceed on Prince St. to the end where New Danville Pike & Route 272 meet by the Conestoga River. Then take New Danville Pike to the village and turn onto Marticville Rd. (Rt. 324 S); go about 3 miles and on your left, up a small rise, stands the one story stone church. This is about 1 1/2 miles from Silver Mines Road, in Pequea Township.

In 1996 the inscriptions were rechecked and data added to Mr. Hess's record. Mr. Hess did not record the cemetery stone by stone, and in his book he re-arranged the order of the rows. He rarely noted the names of the parents and only in a very few stones gave year, month or day.

Many of the stones in the back rows are written in German. These he did not note.

Row 2
Ressel, Murvan C., 1897-1957
Ressel, Martha N. Trissler, his w., 1898-1945
Ressel, Charles, 1874-1964
Ressel, Clara M., 1873-1959
Charles, Benjamin M., 1868-1937
Charles, Annie E., 1869-1956
Charles, Landis W., 1899-1920
Byers, Jacob, 12/27/1803-9/27/1888, 78y10m8d
Byers, Martha, w/o Jacob, 11/8/1808-9/16/1887, 84y11m
McCrabb, Frank, s/o Jacob & Lizzie, 6/30/1882-4/17/1899
McCrabb, Freddie, s/o Jacob and Lizzie, April 22, 189_-3/_/1899
Warren, William W., 1867-1950. Warren, Amelia H., 1869-1957. Warren,
    J. Raymond, 1889-1901
Warren, Paul Lee, 1903-1911
Eshleman, Samuel, GAR A, 9/27/1840-5/23/1888
Eshleman, Mary Hiller, 3/7/1839-
Eshleman, Flora V., no dates
C. S.
F. S.
Brooks, Henry S., father, Co. K 203 Pa. Vol., 4/21/1841-7/18/1910
Brooks, Christiana K., mother, w/o Henry, 4/23/1846-3/30/1932
Brooks, Clara Minnie, 12/14/1876-1/19/1878, 1y2m5d
Brooks, William H., s/o Henry & Christiana, 12/13/1867-4/3/1868, 3m2d
Brooks, Charles A., son, 11/3/1871-1/5/1949
Brooks, Anna, d. 4/17/1879
Brooks, William, 1807-1877. Brooks, Mary, his w., 1817-1892. Brooks,
    Mary A., 1849-1947. Brooks, Jacob, 1838-1839. Brooks, Christian,
    1847-1849
Infant daughters of Henry & Chris, 1875
Hess, Bertha M., d/o Daniel G. & Eliza, d. 9/21/1878, 1m
Weidlich, David L., 1860-1942
Weidlich, Anna M., 1868-1934
Brockway, Henry G. 1850-1926
Brockway, Kate, 1848-1939
Warfel, David, 11/28/1799-2/6/1882, 82y1m8d
Warfel, Margaret S., 8/1/1813-6/10/1898, 84y10m9d
Morton, Benjamin, Co. D 2nd Pa. Cav., 4/7/1843-10/8/1911
Morton, Delia W., 6/22/1850-7/6/1931
Gochenour, S. Elmer, 1876-1947
Gochenour, Mabel F., 1886-1946
Fehl, Jacob W., 1849-1932

Fehl, David W., s/o Jacob & Susan, b/d: 4/3/1916
Miller, Cecelia, 1886-1955
Eshleman, John G. (wife: Mary E. Brooks 2/20/89-8/12/1976), 6/17/1855-3/26/1968
McCrabb, Freddie, s/o Abraham & Lizzie, 11/22/1891-8/28/1899

Row 3
Manning, Abraham S., 1879-1938
Manning, Ruth E., his w., 1875-1945
Bortzfield, Harry K., 10/14/1880-4/29/1966
Bortzfield, Bertha B., his w., 7/14/1885-8/31/1968
Bortzfield, Lois G., dau., 7/7/1909-10/19/1964
Albin, Mary Fehl, 6/15/1883-3/10/1958
Albin, Robert B., f., 4/16/1862-9/29/1930
Clark, Andrew M., f., 1849-1918
Clark, Martha A., m., 1852-1932
Clark, Susan D., dau., 1877-1959
Morton, Benjamin F., f., 1869-1930
Morton, Anna, m., 1874-1963
Morton, Harrison, 1890-1891
Morton, Samuel, 1905-1906
C. S.
D. S.
Beach, Jane W., 10/2/1834-2/8/1918
Beach, Jacob, 4/_/1845-7/3/1907
Beach, Samuel W., f., 8/13/1875-6/21/1957
Tangert, Mary E. Beach, sister, 1867-1944
Beach, Clara W., 1879-1961
Beach, Harry G., s/o Benj. & Lillie, 12/21/1889-2/16/1910, 20y1m6d
Beach, Lillie F., 10/7/1863-7/22/1918, 54y9m15d
Beach, Benjamin F., 1/3/1859-7/18/1928, 69y6m15d
Mayopoulos, Retta H. (Beach), 7/8/1895-12/21/1949
Beach, John H., WWI, US Navy, 1894-1952
Brooks, I. Harvey, f., 1855-1921
Brooks, Alice L., m., 1857-1930
Brooks, Miriam May, d/o I.H. & A., 3/12/1889-3/30/1900, 1y18d
Brooks, Helen E., 1895-1952
Gochenour, Mabel B., 1885-1946, dau. of I.H. & A. Brooks
Brooks, Ira M. s/o I.H. & A., 7/21/1883-2/26/1886, 2y7m5d
Brooks, Benjamin E., s/o I.H. & A., 1/11/1881-2/18/1881, 7m7d
Eshleman, Daniel M., f., 4/19/1853-11/9/1911
Eshleman, Mary A., m., 6/14/1857-4/22/1896
Eshleman, Daniel M., Jr., brother, 12/15/1887-5/10/1912
Eshleman, Eli H., s., 11/11/1881-7/22/1944
Eshleman, infant son, b./d. 9/9/1886

Eshleman, infant son, b./d. 6/4/1882
Eshleman, infant dau., b./d. 6/14/1870
Campbell, Hiram, f., 1844-1923
Campbell, Leah F., m., 1853-1926
Snyder, Sarah J., w/o John, 6/30/1846-3/10/1913
Hess, Daniel, 1850-1924
Hess, Louisa, his w., 1857-1944
Hess, Ora, 1882-1887
Hess, Blaine, 1884-1904
Hess, Earl, 1886-1887
Hess, Robert, 1899-1899
Hess, Clara G, 1879-1919
Hess, Alice, 1888-1906
Hess, Ruth, 1893-1894
M.B.
Cramer, Harold J., brother, 5/21/1903-10/10/1958
Cramer, Edger J., f., 5/27/1877-1/28/1953
Cramer, Anna L., m., 12/18/1880-1/15/1929
Fellenbaum, Clyde S., 11/18/1906-9/17/1965
Fellenbaum, Estella M., his wife, 7/26/1910 -
McClune, Harold E., 1890-1974, Mabel M., 1898-1986, inf. dau. Jean
    Joyce, 1929
Henry, Lillie M., 1908-1970
Henry, Charles E. 1904-1986
Henry, Esta, m. Hess, 1926-1974

Row 4
Beatty, Ira W., 1885-1953
Beatty, Clara E., 1892-1967
Beatty, Flora M., 1915-1976
Beatty, John R. 11/6/1930-2/14/1992. "Johnny The Painter."
Johnson, Jacob H., 1894-1957
Johnson, Mazie M., 1896-1985. Johnson, Helene M., 1921-1925, dau.
Carrigan, Hiram, 3/21/1830-1/25/1902, 70y10m4d
Carrigan, Susanna, wife of Hiram, 12/10/1835-12/19/1913, 78y,9d
McElhaney, D. S., father, 12/21/1821-2/22/1907
McElhaney, Sarah A., mother, 12/22/1820-4/18/1896
McElhaney, W. G., brother, 11/23/1853-7/3/1901
McElhaney, Charlotta A., sister, 2/10/1857-5/20/1912
Hess, Maris K., 7/8/1864-8/21/1950
Hess, Oliva, 3/12/1867-3/11/1924
Hess, Nellie M., d. 1/25/1910
Hess, Barbie M., 2/23/1891-9/9/1898
Hess, H. Franklin, 1862-1950
Rineer, Aaron, 8/3/1833-4/17/1909

Rineer, Margaret, 4/29/1837-6/12/1881
Rineer, Emma F., d/o A. & M., 2/22/1859-1/29/1871, 11y11m7d
Rineer, Eliza Ann, d/o A. & M., 10/14/1866-5/29/1873, 6y7m15d
Rineer, Susan B., w/o Job E., 12/25/1810-3/10/1884
Byers, Henry S., 1871-1954
Byers, Emma L., 1870-1940
Byers, Harry T., 2/1/1893-10/11/1944
Yost, Samuel, 1873-1950
Yost, Henry, f., 4/8/1841-2/9/1922, 80y10m1d
Yost, Rebecca, m., 3/28/1845-12/17/1915, 70y8m19d
Yost, Clayton, son/o Henry & Rebecca, 7/1/1876-5/21/1916, 39y10m20d
J.J.H.
Bookman, Lottie, d/o John & Mary J., d. 12/17/1879
Bookman, John W., 1857-1929
Bookman, Mary J., 1852-1918
Bookman, Minnie M., 9/13/1885-6/25/1904, 18y9m12d
Bookman, John G., of John & Mary J., 10/22/1880-11/18/1880
Bookman, Jessemine, of John & Mary J., b./d. 6/29/1883
Bookman, Miriam, of John & Mary J., 8/23/1903-9/1/1903
Good, Jonas B., 12/5/1842-5/11/1923
Good, Barbara. A., 10/13/1852-9/13/1930
Herr, Emma W., 1910-1990
Herr, Sheriden F., 1905-1990
Shank, Edwin Levi, 7/_/1892-1/_/1899
S.
S.E.S.
Urban, Jeanne M., d/o Clyde E. (1915-1996) & Cecelia H., 4/28/1943-8/28/1943
Wiggins, Edna Carpenter, 1916-
Wiggins, Ross W. Jr., WWII, 1914-1976

Row 5
Charles, John B., 1892-1956
Charles, Lizzie M., 1895-1946
Winters, M. Myrtle, 1889-1969, w/o Wash. C. (1889-1979) (Mason)
Zercher, Betty Mae, 1925-1995
Miller, Lizzie O., 1868-1957
Miller, J. Sheridan, 1865-1940
Ressel, Abbie J., m., 1862-
Ressel, Frank G., f., 1862-1930
Hemperly, Annie M., d/o Elmer & Ida M., 6/21/1893-4/29/1898, 4y10m27d
Hemperly, Earl G., s/o Elmer & Ida M., 5/15/1891-11/26/1904, 13y6m11d
Hemperly, Ida M., w/o of Elmer E., 10/5/1869-3/28/1929
Hemperly, Elmer E., 1/7/1862-6/11/1935
A.M.H.

Hemperly, Ray M. (also infant s/John M.), 8/7/1896-11/26/1918
Hemperly, Sarah, w/o John, 5/28/1802-8/24/1889
Landis, Samuel H., Troop E 11th Cav., WWI, 1899-1954 (Bertha Esther, mother)
Landis, Bertha (no dates)
Landis, Esther (no dates)
Young, Virgie B., 1887-1906. Wm. 1880-1970\Violet 1883-1971
E.R.
H.M.E.
Yost, Rena C., 7/18/1890-4/28/1954
Yost, Harry Y., 3/13/1883-4/24/1966
Ressel, Edith Elva, dau., 1905-1906
Ressel, Eva E. Gainer, wife, 1873-1960
Ressel, Maris B., 1872-1954
Alexander, Jay W., 1935-1982
Barbon, Evelyn May, dau., 1917-1918
Barbon, Russel L., 1891-1921 (Blanche E. Ressel, his wife, 1895-1971)
Neill, infant son, 1914-1914
Neill, Bertha Shoff, his w., 1889-1946
Neill, David, 1885-1933
Heiney, Abrella, 8/22/1851-4/8/1925, 74y
Heiney, Isaac, Co. F 9th Pa. Cav., 4/15/1833-2/23/1912, 79y
Folkman, William, 1874-1936
Folkman, John G., Pvt. USMC, 1877-1940
Kilburn, Lenard C., Co., coxswain, US Navy, d. 1/26/1947
Smith, Minnie Alice, 1872-1953
Smith, Clarence G., 1866-1947

Row 6
Steiner, Benjamin F., 1883-1951, Mable Cremer, his wife, 1887-1972
Steiner, Harry, 1855-1945
Herr, David H., 1878-1961
Herr, Mabel M., 1882-1944
Herr, Clyde R., s/o David H. & Mabel, 6/23/1903-5/16/1922
Herr, Paul L., s/o David H. & Mabel, 1/27/1916-1/8/1920
Herr, John, Co. K 203 Pa. Vol., 5/16/1810-6/15/1908
Herr, Fanny, 6/22/1811-11/11/1911
Herr, Guy A., s/o John & Fanny, 12/12/1931-12/29/1831
Herr, Levi, Co. G 79th Regt., Pa. vol., 1/20/1810-3/30/1890, 80y2m1d
Herr, Leah, w/o Levi, 10/4/1813-6/7/1900, 86y8m3d
Folkman, Christian, 12/23/1835-8/7/1887, 51y7m18d
Folkman, Catharine, w/o Chris, 2/6/1847-5/18/1899, 52y3m12d
Rhinier, Harvey H., 1857-1917
Rhinier, Susan J. 1863-1916
Rhinier, Bertha C., 1900-1978

Landis, Esther Rhinier, 1893-1949
Newport, Amos, 1861-1932
Newport, Sara E. 1859-1941
Newport, Barth E., 1895-1944
Newport, John J., 1887-1919
Newport, Barth A., 1940-1941
Newport, Benjamin E., 1889-1902
Newport, Mary E., 1883-1923
Newport, Amos D. 1890-
Terrell, Grace M., 1/15/1886-10/14/1918
Terrell, Geo. W., 3/12/1883-
Newport, Margaret, w/o John, 1831-1965
Newport, Mary J., 1856-1940
Cully, Sarah E. Newport, w/o Oscar D., d. 1/18/1890, 23 y
Cully, Hettie A., 11/20/1863-4/17/1901, 37y4m27d
Cully, Lee R., brother, 1894-1916
Cully, Florence E., sister, 1897-1924
Brubaker, Barbara, m., 2/17/1829-2/25/1895, 66y3m
Cully, William Bigler, 1868-1951
Cully, Emma Lavina Kendig, 1870-1943
Cully, Mary Naomi, 1901-1954
Rosso, Esther A. Cully, 1895-1930
Fisher, Orceneth Whitney, husband, 6/18/1894-12/25/1929
Brooks, Elsie N. Sterneman,1885-1939, w/o
    Christian H. 1879-1970
Martin, Ralph C., father, 1895-1939
Martin, Raymond, s/o Ralph & Esther, b./d. 10/21/1916
Good, David F., father, 7/6/1859-12/5/1937
Good, Lizzie Urban, w/o David F., 11/10/1860-8/19/1928, 67y8m29d
Good, Hettie M., w/o David F., 9/30.1859-7/4/1890, 30y9m4d
Good, Harry M., s/o David & Hettie M. 10/13-11/6/1882, 24d
McClune, Paul D., 1902-1944
McClune, Emma E. Frymoyer, 1902-1994
Beach, Mary Lorraine McClune, 4/28/1928-6/5/1978, w/o Raymond P.
    Beach, m/o Myron, Nancy & Sandra

Row 7
Spangler, baby girl, 1961-1961
Erb, Helen M., 1900-1964
Erb, Mable E., w/o John, 1892-1943
Erb, John W., 1896-1965
Erb, Daisy O., w/o Harry W., 1886-1926
Erb, Harry W., 1879-1964
Fry, Mary V. Erb, 1905-1995
Herr, Susan M. Aston, 1862-1932

Herr, Joseph H., 1857-1943
Herr, Isabella (w/o John G.), 9/15/1838-1/22/1921, 82y4m7d
Herr, John G., 11/6/183- -5/2/1891, 45y6m20d
Herr, Elvina, d/o John & Isabella, d. 9/28/1877
Herr, Martha E., d/o John & Isabella, 5/28/1867-5/20/1878, 11m2d
Herr, Amos, 3/4/1881-4/7/1883
Herr, Katie M., b./d. 1883
Herr, Charley, 5/22/1871-3/21/1878, 6y2m29d
C.H.
Hemperly, Margie V., w/o Chester, 6/20/1875-6/30/1896, 21y4d
Herr, Mary A., 1842-1923
Herr, Abram, 1839-1926
Ross, infant dau., b./d. 11/3/1899
Ross, Mary A., 10/23/1859-7/29/1911, 51y9m6d, wife of Wm. W. Ross
Ross, William W., 6/20/1855-7/4/1907, 52y68m
Ross, Irene May, 1889-1894, 4y10m11d, d/o W. W. & M.A. Ross
Shoff, Oliver, s/o Henry & Amanda, 4/2/1894-4/23/1895, 1y21d
Shoff, Amanda, w/o Henry, 3/6/1861-4/23/1902, 41y
Shoff, Henry B., 1853-1929
Huber, Elmer, 1906-1984. Esther M., 1907-1979.
Coble, Rose Ann, d/o Walter F. & Rose W., 5/17/1934-6/29/1934
Herr, Annie M., his w., 1870-1937
Herr, Feuben L., 1866-1934
Herr, Elizabeth S., 1895-1916
Herr, Arlean M., 1917-1991
Herr, Clarence S., 1894-1965
Dunn, Eddie R., 1921-1962
Dunn, Winifred H., 1922-1969
Bortzfield, Annie M., d/o Cyrus & Frances, 11/6/1881-4/26/1903
Bortzfield, Martha Frances, 1862-1917
Bortzfield, Cyrus, 1857-1927
Bortzfield, Benj. F., 1880-1881
E. C.
B. C.
Folkman, Charles, 1880-1951
Folkman, Christian B., 1884-1952
Campbell, Ralph L., 3/12/1892-10/21/1918
Herr, Amos, s/o Abr. & Mary, 1881-1883
Herr, Katie M.
Herr, Clara Eva, 3/20/1874-12/6,1878, 5y16d
Bortzfeild, Lloyd G., 1912. Freida E., 1915-1992
Baer, Geo. H., 1915-1988. WWII. Kathryn S., 1924-

Row 8
Herr, John E., 8/5/1862-4/16/1921

Herr, Ida E., w/o John, 7/5/1868-1/10/1929
Herr, Charles B., 1886-1963
Herr, Bertha I., 1886-1924
Herr, Earlna J., 1921-1921
Herr, John D., 1910-1924
Herr, Fay U., 7/27/1912-6/5/1971
Kryder, Jacob, 3/1/1804-3/7/1880, 76y3d
Krider, Charlotte, 12/1/1808-5/8/1882, 73y5m4d
Shoff, Ross, s/o Geo. & Emma L., 5/27/1883-12/28/1887,4y7m1d
Shoff, Jennie Bertha, d/o Henry & Maggie, 7/5/1879-12/5/1889, 10y5m
Shoff, Fredrich H., husband, 9/5/1871-12/17/1899, 27y7m12d
Shoff, Mary E., d/o ___ & S__, 6/3-19/1899
Cully, Kendig Brubake, 11/30/1913-3/29/1987. Iris Virginia, 9/12/1914-
Herr, John E., s/o John G. & Isabella, 4/29/1873-2/14/1901, 27y9m24d
Hess, Emma Frances, 2/1/1863-12/8/1956
Bowman, John W., 1861-1912
Bowman, Delilah Hess, his wife, 1861-1947
Beatty, William M., 1863-1918
Beatty, Maggie M., 1861-1906
Wenzel, Barbara, d/o Fred & Jean, 10/3/1912-1/9/1921
Urban, Joseph W., 1875-1939
Urban, Emma L., w/o Jos. W., 1880-1918
Urban, Jennie M., 1898-1983
Dunn, Robert Eddie, Cpl. 52 Air Base Cap., AF, WWII, 11/29/1922-1/27/1962
E. S.
Heiney, George R., 9/15/1923-7/13/1938
Heiney, George W., GAR Co. D, 1st Reg. Pa., Res. Inf., 12/4/1838-4/2/1916, 77y3m28d
Heiney, Elizabeth, w/o George, 12/1/1845-11/20/1907, 61y11m19d
Heiney, Beulah Mary, gch. of G.W. & Lizzie, 3/3/1894-10/17/1896, 2y7m14d
Heiney, Walter Blaine, s/o G.W. & Liz, 2/11-8/24/1891, 6m13d
Heiney, David S., Co. H 203 Reg. Pa. Inf., 5/5/1803-6/4/1880, 77y24d
Heiney, Fanny, 1/1/1798-9/20/1871
Heiney, Fanny, w/o David S., 1/11/1798-9/20/1871, 73y8m9d
Hess, Wm. C., 1962-1972

Row 9
Farmer, Mary S., 1868-1955
Farmer, Frances S., 1903-1989
Huber, Chas., S., 1885-1978
Huber, Doris F., 1896-1987
Shoff, Jacob H., 1883-1963
Shoff, Susie, sister, 1885-1929

Shoff, Clara, sister, 10/12/1874-8/30/1876
Shoff, Mary E., 5/19/1900-20/1900
Shoff, Elizabeth, sister, 5/30/1873-7/23/1898
Shoff, Annie M., sister, 1868-1947
Shoff, Abraham L., brother, 1866-1936
Shoff, George B. McCleland, brother, 8/14/1865-12/8/l1912
Shoff, Mary E., m., 12/28/1846-11/21/1905
Shoff, Henry, f., 2/18/1829-1/2/1902
Mehaffey, Walter L., 9/12/1867-3/4/1869, 4y5m9d
Mehaffey, Emma Susan, d/o James & Cath., 1/29/1863-1/12/1875, 11y11m16d
Mehaffey, Catharine E., m., 10/17/1830-7/14/1907
Mehaffey, James, f., 6/4/1828-6/17/1875, 47y13d
Good, infant, s/o Ezra & Celia, b./d. 7/4/1894
Good, Lloyd L., s/o Ezra & Celia, 8/28-11/28/1885
Good, Mary E., d/o Ezra & Celia, 5/28/1888-7/25/1892
Good, Cora E.,1877-1969
Good, Martha, m., 8/3/1851-1/12/1906
Good, Martin H., f., 7/7/1855-6/20/1924
Bonholtzer, Bessie C., w/o John, 1/15/1893-3/4/1917
Eshleman, Elizabeth, w/o Walter M., 6/22/1870-1/20/1910
Eshleman, Stella Mae, 1880-1956
Eshleman, Walter M., 1868-1949
Eshleman, Ezra, 1873-1935
Eshleman, Harriet H., m., 11/24/1839-4/26/1921
Eshleman, Martin H., f., 8/31/1841-11/6/1916
Eshleman, Clyde S., son, 1890-1951
Eshleman, Bertha C., m., 1868-1949
Eshleman, Harry M., f., 1865-1929
C.C.
Myers, Verna M., 1918-1924
Myers, Meril E., 1921-1923
Myers, Ruth L., 1920-1921
Myers, Lydia E. Miller, w/o Eugene, 1892-1967
Myers, Eugene E., 1891-1953
Rombach, Linda A. (Myers), w/o Robt. E. Rombach, 1/20/1940-3/24/1968
Myers, Harold B., 5/29/1913-2/17/1972
Myers, Arlene D., 11/23/1916-9/18/1980

Row 10
Huber, Rose M., 1907-1958
Huber, Merle S., s/o Merle W. & Rose, "Buddy", 1928-1946
Aston, Raymond Victor, 1892-1967
Aston, Barbara, 1920-8/22/1936
Herr, Levi, 1850-1912

Herr, Mary, 1842-1915
Herr, Henry C., 1873-1874
S. E.
E. H.
Lehman, Jacob S., GAR, 1829-1879
Lehman, Jacob, 4/16/1796-5/7/1874, 78y21d
Weidlich, Ernest M., GAR, f., 11/14/1823-6/1/1891
Weidlich, Catharine, 11/14/1823-8/13/1884
Aston, Amos K., 1851-1920
Aston, Barbara E., 1852-1937
Aston, Walter W., s/o Amos, 12/25/1884-6/21/1910
Aston, John D., s/o Amos & Barbara, 1/19-11/21-1878
Eshleman, Eli, f., 4/28/1825-12/24/1891, 66y7m
Eshleman, Susan, m., 10/16/1824-1/18/1916, 91y3m2d
Foutz, Miller M., 9/7/1881-12/27/1893, 33y3m20d
Eshleman, Martin M., f., 1851-1933
Eshleman, Angelina, m., 1857-1940
Eshleman, Joseph, 1871-1947
Eshleman, Kate B. Handel, 1879-1953
Eshleman, Benjamin M., 1905-1905
Eshleman, Emma, 1908-1908
Eshleman, Frank H., 1911-1913
Nixdorf, Laird F., 111th Inf. Co. D 28th Div., 1899-1957
Newcomer, Benjamin H., 10/30/1874-3/23/1919
Newcomer, Clara E., 2/11/1878-2/24/1954
Eshleman, Robert Lee, 1921-1921
     s/o C.H. 1895-1977 & Emma 1899-
Yenner, Conrad, 10/28/1886-5/4/1950
Weaver, John Mark, 7/30/1922-6/12/1965
Weaver, Rhoda E., 9/2/1924-

Row 11
Boatman, Florence, 1892-1963
Boatman, Dewey S., 1898-
Andre, John A., WWI, 1897-1956
Andre, Ruth L., 1901-1975
Trout, George M., 1918-. Geneva, 1923-. Donald, 1945-.
Huber, Henry, 10/19/1815-1/20/1885, 69y3m1d
Huber, Anna, 3/5/1821-2/1/1897, 75y10m26d
Huber, Martha, d. 8/28/1840
Huber, Mary Ann, d. 2/2/1844
Huber, Eliza, d. 4/4/1845
Huber, Henry, [Very worn; it may read 2/6/1840-2/20/1840 or 3/6/1840-
     320/1840.]
Shank, Sallie E., d/o Alf & Eliz., 4/6/1858-7/19/1861,-y-m-13d

Shank, Martin H., s/o Alf & Eliz., 9/11-18/1851, 7d
Shank, Clara E., d/o Alf & Eliz., 5/10/1875-8/24/1876,1y3m14d
Shank, Irwin H., s/o Alf & Eliz., 11/20/1871-3/24/1887, 15y7m1d
Shank, Elizabeth, 10/27/1833-7/12/1912
Shank, Alfred, 1/26/1828-4/17/1895
Lee, Alice R., 2/26/1860-5/19/1916
Good, Abran Mylin, 6/30/1870-8/25/1870, 1m25d
Good, John Sherman, s/o John & Eliz., 8/7/1866-2/12/1868, 4y6m5d
Good, Maris M., s/o John J. & Eliz., 1/15/1860-3/30/1860, 2m15d
Good, Thaddus D., s/o Henry & Mary, 11/11/1860-4/10/1862, 1y4m29d
Good, Henry D., Co. I 11 Regt. Pa. Cav., 8/4/1824-11/1/1864, 40y27d
Good, Aaron, 1846-1928
Good, Elizabeth, w/o Joseph, 3/18/1797-9/25/1870, 73y6m7d
Good, Joseph, 1/5/1780-3/17/1871, 93y2m12d
Kneisley, Emma Lizzie, 9/19/1867-4/17/1874, 13y6m28d

Row 12
Turner, Albert L., 1912-1959
Turner, Ethel L., 1918-
Appel, Harry S., 11/12/1933-7/2/1950
Appel, James A., 10/4/1930-8/6/1931
Appel, Mary E., 2/15/1903-
Appel, John, 1/20/1894-
Good, Jonas, s/o John & Veronica, 11/18/1838-1/7/1853, 22y4m20d
Good, Infant son of John V., b./d. 5/17/1833
Herr, John, 11/26/1802-12/28/1870, 68y2d
Herr, Abigail, w/o John, 9/27/1798-7/8/1871
Herr, Sarah Jane, d/o John & Abigail, d. 11/4/1818, 11y9m15d
Herr, Jacob P., f., 5/12/1826-7/7/1899, 73y2m25d
Herr, Annie, w/o Jacob P., m., 5/14/1823-10/9/1904, 81y4m25d
Good, Mary, w/o Jacob K., 12/7/1818-9/2/1891, 72y8m25d
Good, Jacob K., 3/6/1815-7/2/1896, 81y3m26d
Pickell, Cathrine, w/o Isaac Pickell, 3/19/1845-6/21/1884
Good, Abraham H., s/o Mary & Jacob K., 10/8/1843-2/15/1874, 20y1m7d
Good, Joseph H., s/o Mary & Jacob K., 10/6/1862-3/13/1944, 21y21d
Good, John, s/o Mary & Jacob K., 3/29/1832-8/10/1832, 5m
Lehman, Cathrine, w/o Jacob, d/o Felix & Catherine Swigart, 7/12/1793-
    12/5/1867
Eshleman, Henry, s/o Eli & Anna, 1847-1851, 3y9m16d
Eshleman, Sarah, d/o Eli & Susanna, 8/7/1850-12/4/1851, 1y3m28d
Shoff, Christiana, w/o Sam, d/o Jas., & Cath. Lehman, 10/14/1835-
    9/24/1865, 29y11m10d
A.M.G.
Good, Elizabeth H., 6/20/1845-1/8/1929
Good, Mary H., 12/8/1848-1/3/1929

Good, Cathrine, 12/7/1850-12/23/1921
Lynes, Barbara Good, 6/16/1853-12/31/1938
E.S.
H.C.S.

Row 13
Thomas, Barbara, d/o John & Cathrine, 5/25/1839-5/31/1839
Shoff, Infant son/o Mary & Fred
Shoff, Jacob, 8/15/1841-7/3/1843, 1y11m
Shoff, John, s/o Fred & Mary, 9/23/1846-10/7/1849, 3y14d
Shoff, Abraham, s/o Fred & Mary, 1/11/1844-10/13/1849, 5y9m
Shoff, Frederick, s/o Fred & Mary, 5/5/1852-3/31/1853, 11m26d
Shoff, Frederick, 9/17/1810-10/9/1851, 41y22d
Shoff, Mary, w/o Fredr., 5/11/1812-6/1/1884
Fehl, Esther, w/o Jacob, 9/3/1793-11/3/1823
Fehl, George W., d. 9/19/1856, 2y2m21d
Fehl, Henry P., d. 4/10/1848, 4y4m1d
Fehl, Sabena, d/o David & Hannah, d. 7/25/1850
Fehl, Aaron, s/o David & Hannah, 7/3/1852-9/22/1852
Fehl, Hannah W., w/o David, 1/1/1819-1/19/1904, 85y18d
Fehl, David, 7/14/1819-1/16/1891, 77y5m22d
Pyfer, infant son/o ___ & Mildred, b./d. 12/15/1850
Pyfer, Christian, s/o Geo. & Mary, d. 8/26/1831
Pyfer, Elias, s/o Geo. & M., 7/21/1852-12/29/1852
Pyfer, Henry, s/o Geo. & M., d. 11/_/1853
Pyfer, Benjamin, s/o Geo. & Mary, d. 8/19/1856
Pyfer, Mary, d/o Godfred & Anna, 9/16/1849-8/14/1861, 11y7m
McCardle, Cathrine Christina, d/o Wash. & Rach., 4/1/1855-11/2/1859,
    4y7m
McCardle, Jacob L., s/o Wash. & Rach., 10/1/1849-9/6/1870, 20y10m25d
McCardle, Rachael, w/o Washington McArdle, 12/25/1826-10/31/1871,
    44y10m6d
Walter, Jacob, s/o Jacob & Cath., 1/16/1856-8/28/1858
Walter, Catharine, w/o Jacob, m., 3/18/1828-9/3/1903
Walter, Jacob, f., 1829-1910
Cully, William B., Jr., Mason, 1905-1961
Cully, Bertie S., 1876-1966
Cully, Oscar D., 1864-1955
Raihl, Walter L., 1917-1975
Reihr, ___, 6-1976
Cummings, Emma K., 1/16/1896-4/28/1972
Cummings, Geo. J., 8/3/1899-
Cummings [5 unnamed infant stones]
Fryberger, John H., 1918-1978

Row 14
Rhinier, Lou Marie Resch, 1928-1951
Eshleman, Anna, w/o David, d.5/5/1845, 28y9m11d
Shoff, Jacob, f., 7/28/1819-5/30/1876, 56y
Shoff, Elizabeth, w/o Jacob, m., 11/15/1824-6/5/1874, 49y6m20d
Shoff, Abraham, s/o Jacob & Eliz., 12/30/1850-2/16/1869, 18y1m16d
Shoff, Martha Jane, d/o Jacob & Eliz., 1/2-2/11/1854, 1m12d
Shoff, George, brother, 7/6/1824-1/1/1898, 73y5m28d
Shoff, Frederick, 1775-3/3/1843, 68y1m25d
Shoff, Isabella (Armstrong), w/o Fred, d.7/10/1851, 61y
Shoff, Margaret J., d/o Fred & Isabella, d/3/6/1858, 26y1m2d
Shoff, John, brother, 3/13/1809-7/7/1881, 72y9m25d
Shoff, Abraham, brother, 10/27/1817-7/12/1896, 78y8m15d
Miller, Benjamin F., s/o B__ & S__, 9/15/1861-12/16/1861
Miller, Martha E., 8/13/1862-8/6/1863
Harman, Martha Eliz., 10/29/1857-3/22/1858
Lipp, Benjamin, 8/26/1836-2/2/1853
F.S.
Bushum, William, 3/1/1816-9/11/1841, 25y10d
Stouter, Anna, 1/16/1840-3/19/1956
___,___, blank slate
Brooks, Harry E., 1882-1965
Brooks, Orie E., 1883-1952
Miller, Leah A. R. Reese, 1897-
Miller, Lewis C., 1897-1972
Gochenaur, Annie C., 1892-1972
Gochenaur, Arron F., 1889-1972
Rhinier, Edna M., 9/29/1900-5/17/1974
Rhinier, Harvey H., 5/29/1905-8/7/1974
Resch, Edward L., husband, 1927
Resch, Lou Marie Rhinier, wife, 1928-1951
Rhinier, Edith R., mother, 1898-
Rhinier, Daniel S., father, 1897-

Row 15
A.W.S./S./L.E.K./M.E.M.
___, Elmer, s/o ___ & Cath., 3/_/1865, 11d
Hess, Henry A., 3/16/1856-8/8/1956
Stack, Mary, d. 12/11/1833, 4d
Stack, Henry Clay, s/o, d. 8/23/1840, 26d
Stack, Elizabeth, d/o Henry & Cath., d/9/16/1843, 8y10m15d
Henry, Benjamin, d. 5/13/1852, 3w3d
Lipp, Barbara, 7/16/1833-9/4/1833, 6w5d
Lipp, Mary, d/o Christop. & Magdal., 11/2/1831-9/18/1832, 10m16d
Stoner, Christian, 1796-10/_/1832, 36y8m2d

Hiney, David, 7/19/1777-3/3/1872, 94y7m20d
Warfel, Abraham W., d. 8/7/1843, 23y3m
Stauffer, Abraham W., s/o A___ & Maria, 12/12/1836-2/26/1859, 22y4m4d
Warfel, George, 8/10/1792-4/13/1876, 83y8m3d
Warfel, Barbara, w/o Geo., 11/4/1797-9/12/1885, 87y10m8d
Good, Daniel, 4/5/1804-8/1/1863, 59y4m
Good, Elizabeth, w/o Daniel, 12/12/1808-1/25/1878, 69y1m13d
Good, Maris, s/o Dan & Eliz., 10/4/1841-6/11/1846
Good, Adam, s/o Dan & Eliz., 10/4/1841-5/24/1843
Good, Elizabeth, d/o Dan & Eliz., 5/7/1834-4/8/1882
Dietrich, Mary, d/o Tobias & Mary, 1832-9/19/1836, 4y1m16d

Row 16
Wade, Grace V., 1918
Shultz, David H., WWII, 1915-1958
Shultz, Jean Louise, d/o David & Grace, 12/21/1951-12/24/1951
Zercher, Andrew J., 1906-1951
Zercher, Helen M., 1908-
Nelson, Edward, 8/19/1820-12/28/1879, 59y1m9d
E.M.
Sweigart, George W., f., 4/5/1822-10/9/1878, 56y6m1d
Sweigart, Martha A., m., 11/14/1816-6/23/1893, 77y7m9d
Sweigart, Felix, War of 1812, 9/13/1797-10/4/1869, 72y15d
Sweigart, Cathrine, w/o Felix, d/o John & Mary Bostick, 6/24/1799-10/4/1866
Sweigart, Edward M., s/o Geo. & Martha, 6/4/1849-8/12/1852
Sweigart, George W., s/o Geo. & Martha, 8/20/1851-8/5/1852
Sweigart, Felix, s/o Geo. & Martha, 6/30/1847-9/11/1851
Sweigart, Cathrine, d/o Felix & Cath., 6/7/1840-10/11/1849
Sweigart, Mary, w/o Felix W. Sweigart, d/o Felix & Catharine, 10/25/1827-2/18/1849 [Note: He m. a cousin.]
Sweigart, Cathrine, d/o, 9/16/1847-6/24/1848
Sweigart, Felix, s/o, 8/17/1838-3/13/1843
Sweigart, John, s/o, 7/16/1831-5/30/1832, 9m23d
Sweigart, Jacob, s/o Felix & Cath., b./d. May 1833, 10w
Lehman, Eugene E., 1857-1941
Lehman, Martha M., 1862-1949
Beatty, Silas, 3/5/1814-2/10/1885, 70y11m5d
Beatty, Mary, w/o Silas, 11/12/1814-4/20/1901, 80y5m18d
Kreider, Elizabeth (Lehman), 1835-1911
Young, John C., 1891-1940
Young, Iowa E. Boatman, his w., 1894-1962
Young, Carl, d. 12/27/1929
Young, Mandi H., 10/29/1887-11/8/1946
Young, Thomas B., 12/20/1877-7/21/1937

Zehman, Edmund, 1885-1977

Row 17
Charles, James Leroy, s/o Aldus & Jean, 1957-1957
Charles, Kenneth P., 1959-1959
McGraw, Caroline, 1908-1952
McGraw, Albert L, 1914-
Bortzfield, Clyde, 1911-1952
Bortzfield, Annie, 1906-
Pfeiffer, Frederick, 1812 marker, 2/22/1788-12/14/1845
Pfeiffer, Mary, w/o Fred, 8/24/1794-5/4/1848, 56y8m11d
Schweicker, Felix, 7/16/1765-3/20/1826, 60y8m3d
Schweicker, Christinna (Schwenk), 4/22/1768-2/3/1821, 52y9m12d
Baxter, Mercy, 1802-1802
___, Cathrine, 3/22/1774-12/14/1822
Schweicker, Sebastian, Rev. War, 11/15/1736-3/19/1808, 76y1m4d
Sweicker, Agnes Marie, frau. Sebas., 12/22/1743-8/25/1812, 68y1m5d
    [inscription in German]
Schaffer, Johannes, 9/2/1769-4/29/1813, 50y7m27d

Row 18
Groff, baby boy, 1968-1968, 1975-1975
Brooks, Pauline M., 1926-1963
Brooks, Bertram N., 1924-
Wiederrecht, Lloyd G., Pvt. Co. C 30th Inf., WWI, 1901-1958
Wiederrecht, Maria C., 1904-
Seabrooks, Jesse, s/o James, d. 3/15/1805, 7w6d
Seabrooks, Esther, d/o William & Agnes, d. 12/12/1815
Seabrooks, James, d. 12/11/1854, 55y
Kege, Abraham, 5/2/1726-11/8/1784, 58y6m
Kege, Anna, 1727-1768
3 roughly carved stones: 1777/Breneman, ___. ??. 1782/__/1st Alt 49??
Shoff, Frederick, 10/19/1732-11/20/1800, 68y1m1d
Shoff, Magdalena, 1/5/1739-1/17/1804, 67y12d
Yingling, George, f., 1/26/1840-3/3/1921. GAR
Yingling, Esther A., w/o Geo., m. 10/20/1847-8/14/1878
Yingling, Emma, 1/24/1878-6/23/1878
Yingling, Emanuel, 1878-1880
Yingling, Mary Jane, d/o of G. & E., 10/26/1869-7/14/1872
Yingling, Lydia Ann, d. 10/11/1879
Young, Samuel, 1854-1941
Young, Barbara A., 1859-1945
Young, Henry, 1886-1961

Row 19
J.K.C.
Schmidt, Henrich, 1734-1809
Schmidt, Jacob, 3/6/1738-12/13/1801, 63y9m10d
Schmidt, Magadalena, 1753-1831
Smith, Jacob, d. 2/23/1818, 78y6m26d
Schmith, Johannes, 12/30/1775-8/14/1788
Miller, Abraham, 9/_/1755-11/_/1828
Miller, Veronia, 12/11/1761-12/21/1829
Gall, Martin, s/o Heinrich & Eliz., d. 10/19/1826
Gall, Heinrich, 5/_/1771-11/_/1826
Schmeltz, Jacob, 6/5/1791-7/21/1828, 37y1m16d
Eshleman, Samuel, 2/3/1830-7/5/1908. GAR
Eshleman, Cora E., d/o Sam & Mary A., 8/23/1876-8/8/1878
Eshleman, Maris C., s/o Sam & Mary A., 6/7/1867-3/28/1868
Eshleman, Sarah Ann, d/o Sam & Mary A., 3/4/1860-10/10/1863
A.H.
Plank, John J., f., 12/30/1842-9/9/1916, 73y8m9d. GAR
Plank, Mary A., w/o John, m., 12/15/1847-4/5/1910, 62y3m20d
Plank, Clement, s/o John & Mary, 7/25/1879-6/17/1885
Barr, Nathaniel S., husband, 2/2/1846-12/9/1873

Row 20
Price, Holly Ann, dau., 11/19/1952-5/9/1965
Kleinhans, Roy, 1906-1962
Kleinhans, Pearl E., 1911-1966
Sweigart, Edmund, s/o Ed & Mary, 3/1/1813-5/9/1819
C.L.
Sweigert, Henry, 11/11/1815-2/11/1861, 45y3m21d
J.S.
Hemperly, Edgar G., brother, 1/11/1881-10/15/1928
Hemperly, Louisa, w/o Alex. G., mother, 6/22/1838-10/3/1924
Hemperly, Alexander G., f., 11/20/1837-]8/12/1908. GAR
Hemperly, Charles B., s/o Alex. & Louisa, 6/12/1875-10/17/1876
Hemperly, Harry M., 8/3/1874-10/7/1878
Hemperly, Ida L., 5/27/1866-3/8/1868
Hemperly, Emma L., d/o Alex. & Louisa, 12/11-25/1864
Hemperly, L. Eva, sister, 2/21/1869-3/25/1941

Row 21
Shank, Jacob, 7/29/1811-7/2/1852, 40y10m4d
Shank, Fanny, w/o Jacob, 11/8/1810-9/8/1891, 80y10m
Shank, David, Pvt. Hebble Pa., Cav., d. 1928. GAR
McCardel, Susanna, d/o John & ___, 1/29/1821-11/5/1861
McCardel, John, 2/15/1790-5/9/1852

Stauffer, Barbara, d. 1765
Stauffer, Johanne, d. 1759
Stauffer, Christian, 1727-1727?
Stauffer, Jacob, 1737 -
Stauffer, Johanne, 2/22/1722-11/28/l1798
Stauffer, Margaret, _/24/1727-10/19/1799

Row 22
Miller, Elizabeth, w/o Martin?, 2/29/1805-3/1/1833
Miller, Mary, w/o Martin, 1797-5/14/1826
Schenck, Christian, 1/14/1719-2/22/1803, 83y2m12d
Schenck, Barbara, 10/12/1723-1/16/1803, 79y9m5d
Good, Peter, 1/22/1778-5/11/1837
Schenckin, Anna, 1759-12/24/1783. Sister
Good, Peter, d. 1746
Good, Margaret, d. 1760
Good, Johannes, d. 1762
Good, Peter, 1/7/1773-3/10/1785, 42y2m5d
Good, Barbara, w/o Peter, 11/_/1744-4/18/1834, 89y5m
Brenneman, Barbara, nee Schenokin, 1753-1803, 49y5m10d
Good, Cathrine, d/o John, d. 2/18/1812
Good, Mary/ w/o John, 5/13/1773-1/18/1828, 54y9m3d
Good, John, 7/18/1770-4/8/1852
Good, ___, w/o John, 9/13/1781-3/23/1829
Good, Elizabeth, 5/3/1783-8/1/1852
McAlargin, Amos, d. 1811
Eshleman, Jacob, 12/21/1836-7/10/1865
Eshleman, Maria, w/o Jacob, 6/27/1827-9/20/1865
Eshleman, Susanna, d/o Jacob & Maria, 12/15/1851-2/28/1864
Eshleman, David, s/o Jacub & Maria, 7/4-18/1856
Eshleman, David, 4/1/1832-3/22/1863, 29y9d
Eshleman, Rachel, w/o David, d/o Jacob & Susan Harman, 2/23/1804-
    8/22/1828, 23y1m5d
Charles, Pauline R., 5/22/1922-
Charles, Benj. H., 7/2/1917-11/19/1935
Baker, Edw. O., 1893-1973
Baker, Catherine E., 1898-1973
Martin, Donald J., 1843-1970

Row 23
Stauffer, Jacob, d. 1778
Huber, Elinda, w/o Joseph, d/o Henry & Mary Eshleman,
    2/27/18___1/10/1852, 21y10m11d
Good, Abraham, s/o John & Prudens, 3/23/1784-11/4/1784, 7m11d
Good, Jacob, s/o Johan & ___, 5/_/1798-8/_/1793, 3m9d

Good, Johan, 11/_/1769-4/_/1820 [in German]
Grebell, ___, d/o Jacob & Anna, 2/28/1805-11/2/1810
Miller, Abraham, 10/_/1793-6/_/1827, 4y7m22d [in German]

Row 24
Alexander, Purdence, w/o John, 1794-10/2/1873
Harnish, Joseph, 4/23/1788-4/26/1821
Warfel, Henry, s/o Daniel & Magdalena, 12/21/1827-12/28/1829
Warfel, Elizabeth, d/o Daniel & Magdalena, 4/17/1834-10/14/1834
Bushum, Sarah Ann, 7/19/1856-5/7/1858
Good, John K., 4/20/1821-8/8/1867, 41y3m11d
Good, Susan E., m., w/o John, 9/8/1822-7/18/l1895, 72y10m10d
Good, Henry E., s/o John & Susan, 3/5/1857-6/4/1887
Good, Calvin, 7/1/1861-9/13/1861
Good, Cathrine, d/o John & S., d. 3/16/1860
Good, Joseph, s/o John & S., 12/16/1852-4/11/1857
Good, infant son, s/o John & S., b./d. 8/3/1844
Good, Susan

Row 25
Huber, Anna, w/o Fred., 1820-7/26/1895, 75y
Huber, Frederick, 1828-1878
Huber, John, 1817-12/16/1833
Huber, Mary, 7/_/1831-1/3/1832, 5m22d
Huber, Magdalena, w/o Abram., 1797-2/23/1824, 27y8m8d
Huber, Mary, mother, w/o Abram, 8/16/1798-9/7/1886, 88y2d
Huber, Abraham, 2/6/1793-2/4/1858, 64y4m28d
Kryder, Barclay, 10/23/1852-1/6/1875, 22y2m13d
M.P.
Krider, Susan, w/o Jacob, 1780-11/22/1839, 59y11m4d
Krider, Jacob, 1778-5/21/1845
Eshleman, Maris, s/o ?, 12/19/1843-1/21/1876
Eshleman, Polly, 1/8/1800-2/3/1873
Eshleman, Henry, 6/26/1790-4/30/1855
Eshleman, Calvin, GAR, erected by Kosciusko Lodge, 9/17/1835-
    11/10/1887, 52y1m25d
Smith, Terre, d/o J. Warren & Nancy Smith, 12/23/1964-10/31/1970

MT. NEBO PRESBYTERIAN CHURCH CEMETERY
(Also known as CLARK'S CEMETERY)

This was copied from my record of this cemetery given to Lancaster County Historical Society seven years ago.

Compiled by Jenne & Elaine Hogarth Renkin (Mrs. Wm. M.). Recopied by Jenne Renkin, December, 1978.

Ellis & Evens, *History of Lancaster County, Pennsylvania*, 1883, page 975, gives a short history of the church. Its charter was granted in 1854. The graveyard beside it was called Clark's Cemetery and the first known burial was Wm. Neil - 8 Feb. 1814.

The graveyard is a 14 row yard with many missing tombstones. It sits on a hill by Westview Road which comes off Delta Road 1.5 miles from Mt. Nebo.

James Clark, who d. ca. 1835, owned this land. His son Joseph Clark deeded it to Mary, Grizzale & Sarah J. Clark in 1835. These ladies conveyed the land by deed (Q-8-533) to the Mt. Nebo Presbyterian Congregation on 19 August 1857. It contained 1 acre, 68 perches.

The Congregation was incorporated in 1854 as Clark's Presbyterian Congregation of Martic Township (Deed:G-8-67 to 70).

The two story brick building was dated 1854. I noted on 18 Dec. 1978 that the roof was falling apart. By 1995 the building had disappeared. In 1971 the lot records were in the hands of Amos Erb, RD #1, Pequea, Pa.

Row 1
Railing, Glenn E., 1926-. E. Josephine, 1929-1987
Erb, Franklin W., 11/13/1860-3/19/1917, 56y4m16d
Dunkle, John E., s/o A.S. & Annie H., 9/22/1910-3/29/1911
Dunkle, Helen M., d/o A.S. & Annie H., 3/15/1908-3/22/1911
Dunkle, Annie H., w/o A. Stanley., mother, 11/6/1879-12/7/1911
Dunkle, A. Stanley, father, 7/10/1880-11/7/1918
Brubaker, John, s/o J.T. & E. H., 7/21/-9/3/1916
Brubaker, John T., father, 1857-1928
Brubaker, Emma H., mother, 1852-1922
Warpenstein, Jacob Shickley, 1884-1955
Warpenstein, Susan A., 1889-
Warpenstein, Charles H., 1880-1956
Shickley, Sarah J., mother, 3/19/1855-12/3/1919
Shickley, Eli, father, 2/14/1850-9/18/1926

Campbell, Ire Howard, fther, 1879-1968
Campbell, Anna Erb, mother, 1885-1967
Campbell, Ire E., 1907-1907
Campbell, Clayton E. 1908-1910
Campbell, Edna E., 1910-1915
Campbell, John E., 1919-1924
Campbell, Chester E., 1924-1924
Campbell, Ira E., s/o Ira H. & Anna W., 11/2/1906-2/23/1907
Campbell, Minnie Shoff, sister, 1866-
Campbell, E. Percy, brother, 1874-1954
Campbell, C. Chester, 1876-1956
Arbaugh, Philip [funeral home marker] 1876-1970.
Arbaugh, Clarence P., 1876-1970. Father
Bechtold, Grace Arbaugh, 1894-1989. Mother
J.F.M., this small stone is leaning on wood fence post

Row 2
Hughs, Ellis, s/o Ellis & Susan, brother, 10/25/1865-3/5/1905
Hughs, Ellis, father, 12/29/1827-3/28/1903, 75y2m29d
Hughs, Oron F., s/o Ellis & Susan, d. 1/19/1898, 28y10m8d
Hughs, Susan, mother, 11/4/1829-1/25/1910, 80y2m21d
Buffington, Mary, mother, d. 11/18/1879, 76y
Stone post with J.Clark on s. side; S. Alexander on w. side
Clark, John C., 1871-
Clark, Alice M., his wife, 1871-1920
Clark, Susan A. Markle, w/o Joseph (our sister), 9/3/1848-2/24/1911,
    63y6m23d
Clark, Joseph, GAR, 4/29/1846-2/14/1910, 64y9m15d
Clark, Delilah Gardner, w/o Joseph, d/o J. & L., 7/19/1845-6/22/1883,
    37y11m3d
Stone post with L.E. Jenkins on it
Jenkins, H. Maud, d/o Lewis E. & Mary, 3/3-9/30/1881, 6m27d
Jenkins, Lewis E., husband, 2/15/1849-7/18/1887, 47y4m3d
Jenkins, Mary, w/o Lewis, mother, 5/1/1846-4/6/1921
Campbell, George, 3/21/1821-5/16/1911, 89y1m25d
O'Nail, Mary A., 4/17/1835-12/4/1907, 76y6m17d
Douts, William, 10/16/1814-11/8, 1892, 78y1m2d
Hoopes, Coleman, 9/31/1843-11/19/1916
Erb, John W., brother, 1886-1959
Erb, Edna W., sister, 1889-1973.
Erb, Clayton W., brother, 1888-1938
E.H., E. H., M.H.J., small stone

Row 3
Railing, Alice Mae, daughter, 1914-1918

Railing, John, funeral home marker, 1886-1966
Shenk, J. Andrew, 8/1/1886-10/10/1966. Wife Edna Shenk, 9/28/1889-
9/12/1978. Edna Shenk, 9/28/1889-9/12/1978
D.H., stone post
Hagen, Margaret M., w/o Davis H. Sr., 5/4/1816-5/15/1887
Hagen, David, 11/9/1809-5/6/1880, 70y5m27d
Stone port with S. Aleander on it
Alexander, J. Colin, s/o Samuel & Jennie M., 11/5/1879-9/3/1881, 1y10m
Miles, Lulu M., mother, 1882-1929
Miles, Emanuel, father, 1882-1948
Miles, Russel J., s/o Eman. & Lula, 6/8-1912-5/5/1913
M.A.E. [cornerstone]
Erb, Maria, w/o John, mother, 2/2/1824-9/12/1906, 82y7m10d
Erb, John, father, 8/25/1814-12/31/1894, 80y4m6d
Erb, Clayton, 1858-1931
Erb, Esther, 1863-1931
Erb, Elias W., s/o Clayton & Hettie H., 8/14/1897-12/17/1898, 1y4m3d
Erb, Fanny W., d/o Clayton & Hettie H., 12/7/1895-11/15/1897, 1y11m8d
Erb, infant son, s/o Clayton & Hettie H., d. 8/13/1884
Erb, Enos W., s/o Clayton & Hettie H., 5/7-12/1902, 5 d (broken)
Erb, Mary Jane, sister, 10/8/1854-5/2/1934
Erb, Susan, sister, d. 2/15/1915, 73y8m26d
Erb, Amaziah W., brother, 5/6/1842-6/10/1872, 30y1m13d
Erb, Emanuel W., 7/25/1856-4/21/1892, 35y8m27d
Erb, Dora May, s/o Alduse & Lillie, 1/5/1890-12/7/1893, 3y11m2d
Erb, Aldus E., father, 1865-1942
Erb, Frances E., mother, 1871-1905
Kleinhans, Myrtle, w/o Fred, mother, 1898-1926
Schmidt, John M., 1848-1916
Schmidt, Jacob J., 1885-1956
Schmidt, Emma A., 1854-1927
Schmidt, Suie E., 1885-1952
McLong, Joseph E., 3/29/1857-11/29/1882, 23y8m-

Row 4
Gibson, Mary J., sister, 7/12/1835-8/17/1913
Gibson, Samuel, brother, 3/13/1831-8/17/1906
Gibson, James L., d. 9/1/1883, 55y7m3d
Gibson, Grizzella, w/o James, 8/28/1802-8/24/1876
Gibson, James, 3/26/1791-3/4/1868
Gibson, Robert S., brother, 1844-1861
Pegan, Eleanor M. Gibson, sister, 1836-1915
Erb, Irene M., d/o John & Lettie A., 10/30/1875-6/8/1889, 15y9m8d
Erb, Bertha, d/o John & Lettie A., 10/30/1875-1/_/1878, 3y2m29d
Erb, Letitia Ann, w/o John R., mother, 3/1/850-2/14/1884, 33y11m13d

Erb, John R., father, 7/7/1847-12/26/1882, 35y8m19d
Erb, Edith E., d/o John & Lettie A., _/29/1877-3/21/1879, 2y2m21d
Erb, Albert E., s/o John & Lettie A., 3/22-12/26/1879, 9m4d
Erb, Alice H., d/o John & Lettie A., 12/6/1880-5/5/1892, 11y3m29d
J.M.
Markley, Effie Z., d/o John F. & Kate, 10/28/1878-10/3/1883, 4y11m
Markley, John, father, 3/3/1817-6/27/1891, 71y27d
Markley, Anna, w/o John, mother, 12/26/1816-6/19/1884, 68y8m3d
J.M.
Rhoads, Virginia Brubaker, sister, 1877-1962
Bader, Ada Flowers, 1884-1962
Brubaker, John S., father, 3/8/1861-1/4/1911
Brubaker, Elizabeth, mother, 1/16/1827-9/13/1910
Brubaker, Benjamin, 10/21/1871-7/15/1890, 18y9m3d
Brubaker, Martha, 2/10/1858-9/28/1882, 24y7m18d
Kerr, Elizabeth Brubaker, w/o Argus, 3/22/1868-1/11/1953
Beach, Margaret J., d/o Amos W. & Ada B., 7/26-9/1_/1894, 1m7d
Beach, infant, d/o Amos W. & Ada B., d. 2/23/1896
Beach, Ethel M., d/o Amos W. & Ada B., 4/12-8/23/1898, 4m9d
Beach, infant, d/o Amos W. & Ada B., d. 1902
M.S.
Beach, Amos W., father, 3/17/1871-1/29/1910
Drumm, Peter C., 1860-1920
Drumm, Susan Jenkins, his wife, 1870-1941
Drumm, Leigh V., 1897-1913
Drumm, Elvina Mae, 1908-1913
Sweigart, William, 10/9/1853-8/17/1907
Sweigart, Katie L, w/o Wm., 11/24/1846-
Sweigart, George Leroy, d. 10/18/1895, 12y22d

Row 5
Clayman, Cora I., 7/24/1873-6/23/1879. Clayman, Francina J., mother,
    10/22/1848-4/28/1892. Clayman, J. Winston, 8/24/1876-6/23/1879.
    Clayman, Mary A., 9/5-12/9/1879. [All on same stone.]
Laird, Hugh C., s/o C. & A., d. 10/25/1874, 6y10m20d
Laird, Thomas S., 9/25/1864-8/20/1885
Laird, Willie E., s/o C. & A., d. 1/11/1876, __y8m10d
Laird, Anna, w/o Clarkson, 4/19/1838-8/16/1871, __y2m27d, broken
Laird, Clarkson, 3/29/1831-7/27/1889
Sides, Jacob, 1837-1911
Sides, Rebecca, his wife, 1842-1921
Small stone
T.J.N.
Garber, Mary L. Brubaker, w/o Andrew H., mother, 7/17/1860-2/13/1929
Neel, Catherine, w/o Thomas, mother, 2/6/1817-2/19/1892, 75y4d, broken

Neel, Thomas I., father, 7/11/1810-10/26/1876, 66y3m15d
Porter, Gursella, sister, d. 3/15/1885, 81y4m27d
Neel, James W., brother, 6/19/1813-4/9/1887, 73y__m20d

Row 6
Brubaker, Rolandus, father, 1/10/1827-12/17/1908, 81y11m7d
Brubaker, Mary J. Stewart, w/o Rolandus Brubaker, 7/2/1829-10/19/1897,
    68y3m17d
M.S.
Stewart, Margaret, w/o Thomas, mother, d. 12/8/1888, 78y7m
Stewart, Thomas, father, 1/1/1806-9/13/1880, 74y__m22d
Stewart, Willie, s/o Alirad & Ba___, 10/1/1875-8/2/1876,10m1d
Stewart, Gora A., d/o ___ & ___, 10/20/1880-
Franklin, Ella L. Engle, 1867-1922
Engles, Joseph, father, 1823-1899
Engles, Mary, mother, 1829-1896
Engles, Sarah E., 8/22/1850-4/16/1893, 42y9m24d
Engles, Benjamin L., s/o Mary & Joseph, 2/16/1852-2/17/1872
Engles, Jesse Oblando, s/o Joseph & Mary, d. 12/15/1863, 1y8m17d
Sides, Wilber C., s/o Jacob & Rebecca, 8/10/1874-7/29/1878, 3y11m9d
Sides, Clarkson, d. 4/16/1859, 23y5m2d
Sides, Rebecca, w/o Jacob, d. 4/14/1858
Sides, Jacob, d. 8/4/1855, 61y
R.S., C.S., Wm.McG., W.McG.
Hoopes, Mary McGreary, 1874-1877
McCreary, Emma, d/o James M. & M. E., d. 5/25/1865, 5m2d
McCreary, William, 9/3/1788-8/22/1868, 79y11m20d
McCreary, Elizabeth, 4/10/1785-11/4/1865, 80y6m24d
McCreary, John, 11/8/1771-9/17/1850, 78y10m9d
McCreary, Margaret, 1/20d/1783-4/12/1859, 66y2m2d
McCreary, Walter S., s/o James A. & Annie Hoopes McC., 1872/1873
McCreary, Rebecca, w/o John, d/12/8/1819, 76y
McCreary, John, d/9/1/1816, 85y
Neel, Rebecca, w/o James, d. 6/10/1814, 42y
Neel, James, d. March 24, 1848, 72y

Row 7
Walton, Isaac, 1835-1913
Walton, Hannah, his wife, 1845-1916
Walton, Anna Margie, 6/15/1876-9/3/1881, 5y2m18d
Walton, Amos, Sr., father, 12/12/1803-4/3/1879, 75y3m25d
___, Lewis, s/o ___ & ___, d. 3/2/1870, 2y1m9d
Alexander, Jason, s/o John & Susan, 1/27/1844-4/20/1847, 3y2m23d
Alexander, Susan, w/o John, mother, 9/2/1815-5/23/1880, 64y8m21d
Alexander, John, father, 10/27/1803-12/21/1877, 74y2m4d

Alexander, Maris, s/o John, Co.K 77 Rgt. Pa. Vol., GAR, 1/31/1840-1/16/1862, 21y11m15d
Clark, Sarah Jane, 10/26/1806-1/23/1890, 83y7m27d
Clark, Mary, 1/20/1796-11/10/1882, 86y9m20d
Clark, Grizel, 11/1/1799-10/21/1865, 65y11m20d
Clark, Dorcas, w/o Thomas, broken, 6/23/1808-7/7/1887, 79y10d
Clark, Thomas, 7/2/1803-3/21/1872, 69y4m21d
Clark, B. Franklin, s/o T. & D., d. 2/18/1841, 13y
Clark, Angeline, d/o T. D., d. 3/23/1841, 3y
Clark, Rebecca, d/o T. & D., d. 2/18/1837, 4y
Clark, John, s/o J. & R., d. 3/4/1840, 24y
Clark, Margaret Gibson, d/o Joseph & Recca Clark, d. 5/6/1870, 34y3m13d
Clark, James M., d. 6/9/1837, 27y
Clark, John B., d. 5/25/1831, 34y
D.C.; J.C./S.C.
Clark, James, d. 5/5/1811, 45y
Clark, Sarah, w/o James, d. 8/8/1846, 81y
Clark, William, d. 7/15/1844, 50y
Clark, Joseph, d. 8/10/1845, 44y
Clark, Rebecca, w/o Joseph, mother, 4/18/1808-2/6/1883, 71y9m16d
Neel, William, broken, 12/21/1765-2/8/11813, 48y

Row 8
Clark, James, 1834-1912
Clark, Mary E., his wife, 1835-1918
M.S.P./S.S.P.
Porter, Samuel S., d. 8/3/1886, 82y
S.J.C.
Brubaker, Benj., Co. E, 2nd Pa. Cav. (gov't. stone), GAR, no dates
M.J.S./R.B.
Rice, John B., d. 12/2/1836, 2y7m7d
R. C., broken/ T.G./ M.G./ T.B.
Black, Thomas, d. 5/27/1817, 64y6m8d

Row 9
Akins, James, d. 10/23/1899, 55y
Akins, Mary, d. 2/22/1902, 54y
Pegan, Mary E., w/o James, 8/23/1845-1/10/1927
Pegan, James H., 8/18/1818-1/11/1898, 79y4m23d
Pegan, Harriet, w/o James H., d. 5/20/1874, 49y22d
Pegan, Jane, w/o Andrew, 3/29/1793-12/10/1878, 85y8m11d
Pegan, Harriet Jane, d/o Alex. L. & Beth Jane, 3/27/1850-3/1/1873, 22y11m5d
Pegan, Mary S., d/o Andrew & Jane, 6/16/1825-9/2/1869, 44y2m10d
Nimlow, Margaret, w/o George M., mother, d. 8/31/1878, 62y11m5d

Nimlow, Miller K., s/o George M., brother, d. 7/22/1870, 16y3m18d
Nimlow, Ida Jane, d/o George M., d. 2/16/1861, 4y1m22d
Nimlow, George M., father, d. 6/29/1864, 51y5m28d
___, Olivia, broken, 12/4-26/1889
___, Willie, 11/15-19/1878
Galen, Unetty, d/o Edward & Nancy, d. 8/18/1854, 2y5m16d
Galen, Mary, w/o Henry, mother, 5/5/1817-8/10/1887, 70y3m6d
Galen, Henry, father, broken, 3/15/1806-1/13/1884, 77y69m29d
Galen, Rosanna, d. 6/8,1856, 84y
Galen, James, d. 8/19/1846, 84y

Row 10
Moss, Sarah J., w/o Patrick, mother, 10/3/1834-6/6/1914, 79y8m3d
Moss, Patrick, 10/22/1829-6/8/1891, 61y7m17d
P.M.
Armstrong, Hannah, mother, 2/11/1835-4/8/1910
Armstrong, Hugh, father, GAR, 2/22/1835-9/26/1895
Armstrong, Joseph, uncle, 3/2/1814-1/17/1892, 77y10m5d
Armstrong, Fanny, w/o John, 6/11/1809-3/11/1891, 81y9m
Armstrong, John A., 5/7/1811-8/11/1889, 77y9m4d
Armstrong, Jane Ann, w/o Hugh, d. 5/1/1876, 88y
Armstrong, Hugh, 2/__/1779-4/27/1867, 88y2m
Fulton, Ann, d/o John & Fanny Armstrong, 7/13/1838-8/28/1865, 27y1m8d
Armstrong, Henry, s/o John & Fanny, Co. E 1st Regt. Pa. Rev.,
    Gettysburg, 6/14/1836-7/3/1863, 27y19d
Boreman, Mary, 12/20/1790-10/20/1866
Hoopes, Maris, father, GAR, 8/27/1801-11/12/1878, 77y2m15d
Hoopes, Jacob Thomas, s/o Maris H. & Eliza J. Gainer, 1/6/1867-4/28/1868
Hoopes, Mary Ann, mother, 5/29/1808-7/28/1885, 77y1m29d
Hoopes, 5 small stones, no dates: Elizabeth; Mary; Harriet; Henry; Wm.,
    s/o Maris & Maria
F.M. leaning on tree
___ leaning on tree; only "Leonard & Co.," inscribed on the broken base
    of the stone.
Laird, John, d. 3/13/1849, 72y
Laird, Jane, w/o John, d. 1/23/1850, 67y [d/o John Armstrong]

Row 11
Hagen, Mary, 12/11/1811-12/12/1892, 81y1d
Hagen, Joshua, 12/23/1803-6/2/1883, 79y6m9d
Hagen, Sarah, w/o Elijah, mother, 5/20/1820-3/31/1882, 61y10m11d
Hagen, Elijah, 7/31/1821-6/26/1878, 56y5m26d
Campbell, John, 1839-1904
Campbell, Sarah E., 1847-1931
Campbell, Ida F., 1872-1927

Campbell, E. Alice, 1869-1959
Campbell, J., Co. __ 79th Pa. Inf., Corp'l.
J.M.C./U.C.
Gainer, John, father, 12/14/1804-1/22/1890
Gainer, Elizabeth, mother, 10/23/1804-7/4/1872
W.C.
L?R?G?/J.T.G./G.K.M. 3 small stones
Moore, George Kendig, s/o Samuel & Ruth, d. 3/10/1815, 3y2m14d
Moss, Harriet, w/o John, mother, broken, 3/8/1823-8/16/1890, 73y5m
M.
Moss. James, d. 3/18/1831,33y
Moss, Unity, w/o James, d. 3/11/1852, 52y
J.M./ U.M.
Moss, Felix, d. 3/26/1869, 72y
S.MmC./ M.McC./ C.McC./ S.McC.

Row 12
Cramer, George W., father, 2/10/1856
Cramer, Anna M., mother, 11/16/1861
Cramer, G. Herbert, 1893-1909
Cramer, L.S., 1907
Cramer, Anna E., 1905
Cramer, H. Harrison, 1888-1901
Cramer, H. C., 1900
Cramer, Ellen D., w/o Philip, 3/11/1830-11/11/1886
Cramer, Philip, Co. D 2nd Pa. Cav., GAR, no dates
Cramer, George, father, 1819-1869
Cramer, Mary, mother, 1818-1886
Cramer, George E., son, 1855-1883
J.C./ x, two 1/2 buried stones [now gone]
Uffleman, William, Co. D 122nd Pa. Inf., Corpl., GAR, no dates
J.B.H.
McMcues, Sarah __ [cannot read __ 1856?]
McMcues, Machael, s/o Cornelius & Sarah, d. 10/17/1811, 26y4m6d
McMcues, Sarah, d. 3/21/1851, 66y
McMcues, Cornelius, d. 11/29/1866, 85y3m29d
Jolly, James, 4/16/1830-7/8/1832, 2y3m2d

Row 13
J.D./ M.D.
Dout, Mary, d/o Robert & Janet, d. 4/24/1844, 32y
Dout, Janet, w/o Robert, d. 1/_1/1838, 43y
Dout, Robert, d. 6/30/18__, 69y
Dout, Janet, d/o Robert, d. 12/27/1853, 40y

Heeps, Jane, 1st w/o John B., leaning on stone marked E.O'N., d. 8/__/1835
Heeps, Catherine, 2nd w/o John B., d. 12/23/1866, 56y
Heeps, John B., d. 3/27/1895, 82y5m2d
Heeps, James, s/o John B. & Catherine, d. 10/26/1850, 1y5m7d
J.H./ G.H./ J. H. Small stones
Krow, George W., s/o Geo. W. & Jane ___
    G. W. K. March 12, 1819.
    Infant son died Jan 26th.
Fullerton, J. A., Co. I 20th Pa. Cav., GAR, no dates

Row 14
Walton, Joseph, father, 12/24/1834-1/3/1904, 69y9d
Walton, Annetta C., mother, 9/29/1838-4/4/1916, 77y3m5d
J.M./ S.McD. 2 small stones
Walton, Barbara Ellen, w/o Jesse, d. 1/11/1876, 69y
Walton, Jesse, 2/8/1806-6/1/1873, 67y3m21d
Douts, Maris, s/o George & Lillian, 7/2/1865-11/22/1869, 4y4m20d
McDonnell, Susanna, d. 8/22/1858, 57y
Funk, Mich'l., Co. D 2nd Pa. Cav., GAR, no dates
O'Nieal, Henry, 3/18/11809-12/7/1880, 71y6m30d
O'Nail, Elizabeth, w/o H., 4/3/1813-12/2/1857, 44y1m8d. Mother
Himes, Wm., Co. M 7th Pa. Cav., GAR, d. 1897

MOUNT NEBO METHODIST CHURCH
Compiled by Jenne Renkin, December 1978

The deeds are on file at Lancaster County Courthouse for Mount Nebo Methodist Episcopal Church, Mt. Nebo, Martic Twp., Lancaster Co., Pennsylvania.

Row 1 - starts in front of 3rd window of old (1882) building, going toward the rear.
Erb, Oliver E., father, 7/7/l1878-3/12/1956
Erb, Agnes N., mother, 7/21/1878-12/23/1951
Walton, Elizabeth, mother, 10/11/1854-5/7/1939
Walton, Jesse, father, d. 1/16/1900, 51y
JRH
Campbell, Florence S., d/o Geo. W. & Nancy, 9/30/1888-1/5/1895
Campbell, George W., father, GAR, 11/3/1841-9/25/1919
Campbell, Nancy, mother, 1/1/1852-2/12/1940
Campbell, John W., GAR, 11/8/1885-12/20/1952

Douglass, Robert J., Pvt. Co. A, 9th Rgt. NJ Vol. Inf., GAR, 5/3/1848-3/1/1910
Cramer, Enos, 1879-1963
Cramer, Annie J., 1879-1942
Kreiner, Victorene M. (on same stone with E & A), 1843-1914
Alexander, Mary, d/o Roy & Elizabeth, 1912-1917
Alexander, Erma Mae, d/o Roy & Elizabeth, 1916-1918
Alexander, Roy E., 1889-1978
Alexander, Elizabeth B., 1890-1973

Row 2
Douts, John R., s/o Henry & Annie, 10/16/1884-2/5/1905, 20y3m20d
Douts, Henry, 1855-1915
Douts, Annie, his w., 1856-1936
Winters, Harry C., 5/27/1883-6/19/1893
McMillen, Emma, mother, 1866-1891
McMillen, Joseph A., father, 1867-1935
McMillan, Harry, 4/11/1860-2/22/1891, 30y10m11d
McMillan, Isabella, w/o Harry K., 10/12/1860-11/21/1926, 66y1m9d
McMillan, Gertrude May, d/o Harry & Isa., 12/13/1880-9/21/1896, 15y9m9d
McMillan, Lurella, d/o Harry & Isa., 4/24/1886-7/21/1901, 18y3m7d
McMillan, Mary Rebecca, d/o Harry & Isa., 9/28/1884-8/16/1901, 19y10m18d
Hambleton, B. Kinsey (Rev.), 1834-1916
Hambleton, Emma C., his wife, 1842-1918
Channel, Clarence, s/o Thomas I. & Ida M., 2/10/1899-3/23/1908, 9y1m30d
Alexander, Bertha, w/Emerson B., mother, 12/27/1880-5/28/1912
Alexander, Earl F., son, 7/14/1902-2/19/1927

Row 3 - angles from Row 2 to Row 4
Erb, Louisa C., 1874-1964
Erb, Amer. C., 1896-1904
Erb, Benjamin E., 1867-1897
E. (post); rusting metal post, 5 stones with: A., M., M., M., M.
M.E.A. (small stone)
C.A.C. (small stone)
Ewing, John S., 6/27/1825-12/18/1884, 59y5m21d
J.S.E. (small stone)
M.G.G. (small stone)
E. (post)

Row 4
Crawford, Martha, 12/15/1837-7/21/1917
Crawford, Henrietta, w/o Theophilus, in her 94th y, (no date given)

Crawford, Theophilus, GAR, d. 4/7/1872, 70y
Crawford, Alfred, s/o Theophilus, d. 6/__/18-7, 23y
A.C.
Crawford, Mary C., w/o John, 1810-5/11/1884, 74y
Crawford, John, Co. K 50 Pa. Vol. Mil., GAR, d. 2/23/1895
Alexander, Esther M., w/o John W., 1889-1922
Alexander, John W., 1883-1973
Alexander, Bertha, wife, 10/30/1885-8/27/1908
Alexander, John G., s/o John W. & Bertha, 1908-1914
Gainer, William H., 1858-1939
Gainer, Adaline Keens, his wife, 1861-1947
Gainer, W. Henry, Jr., 1895-1961
Gainer, Eva E., his wife, 1899-1972

Row 5
Morrison, Joseph E., 1861-1940
Morrison, Emma F. Hill, his wife, 1870-1941
Morrison, infant sons, 1893-1893, 1907-1907
JLE
Alexander, Elizabeth, d/o Thomas & Hannah, 11/9/1827-7/7/18-6, -
    0y1m24d
Clark, Dwight L., son, 1882-1929
Clark, Joseph B., father, 1857-1921
Clark, Daniel L., son, 1884-1916
Clark, Rebecca M., w/o Joseph B., mother, 1850-1890
Camp, Grace, inf. d/o W. A. & Jennie, d. 12/25/1890, 2d
Camp, Jennie, w/W.A., 9/16186- -9/3/189-, 27y11m7d
Morrison, W. Howard, s/o Matthew & Grace (brother) 1874-1895
Zappulla, Samuel, s/o Benj., 2/31/1913-5/22/1914

Row 6
Campbell, Mary, w/o John, d/8/5/1883,67y6m3d
Campbell, John, d. 6/20d/1889, 85y7m9d
M.C.
Armstrong, Clarence F., s/o Thom. & Annie, 3/22-12/5/1890, 8m13d
Armstrong, Myrtle, d/o Thom. & Annie, b/d 4/17/1892
Armstrong, Mary Edith, d/o Thom. & Annie, 2/14/1894-1/5/1895, 10m21d
Armstrong, Annie M., w/o Thomas, 12/19/1853-10/11/1908, 54y9m22d
Armstrong, Thomas, 2/16/1851-5/20/1933, 83y3m4d
Armstrong, Annie S., w/o Thomas, 9/10/1869-10/23/1919, 50y1m13d
Hart, Susan, w/o Jacob, 12/1/1828-7/14/1906
Hart, Jacob, 5/29/1825-3/11/1904
Hart, Jasper R., s/o Jacob & Susan, 4/24/1849-3/22/1874, 21y11m29d
Hart, Willie, s/o Jacob & Susan, can not read child size stone
Hart, Kate A., d/o Jacob & Susan, can not read child size stone

Hart, Nancy, d/o Jacob & Susan, can not read child size stone
Hart, Hariet M., d/o Jacob & Susan, can not read this child size stone
K.E.H.
Lan__, Josie H., s/o Abram Lan- & Lizzie W. Gerlock, 2/12/1891-2/3/1895
Tomlinson, Rickey W., s/o Willard & A. Jane, 7/7-9/1953

Row 7
Massey, Eliza Ann, w/o Isaac N., d. 11/6/1896, 62y7m21d
Massey, Isaac, GAR, d. 10/12/1896, 61y
Alexander, David, 1834-1900
Alexander, Lucinda, 1835-1902
Neill, John B., 1857-1918
Neill, Kate L., same stone, 1858-1889
Neill, Clarence B., 1883-1899
McCue, Nancy, w/o James, d. 1/2/1902, 87y
McCue, James, GAR, 1809-4/30/1886, 77y
Lines, Sarah, d. 8/11/1851, 9y1m8d
Girvin, Chester T., 1894-
Girvin, Mabel, same stone, 1895-
Girvin, Marvin M., b/d 1918
Girvin, Martha E., d/o Merle & Naomi, b/d 7/26/1948
Girvin, Martin M., s/o Chester & Mabel, b/d 1918
Patton, Linnie M., mother, 1873-1943
Patton, Oliver C., father, 1868-1926
Karr, John W., father, 1896-1923
Karr, Ethel M. Patton, mother, 1895-1918, daughter
Kauffman, Jessie Wood, w/o J. Edward, 1917-1952

Row 8
Crawford, Lydia, w/o W. A. & d/o J. M. Bookman, d. 12/26/1885, 21y10m
Greist, Isaac, father, d. 3/18/1876, 77y
Greist, Margaret Ankrim, w/o Isaac Griest, mother, d/11/1/1879, 75y
McEli-ney, old stone, 8/13/1820-8/19/1842, 22y6d
Rice, Peter, old stone, d. 4/12/1842, 66y
___, Mary, old stone, 6_y
T.A.
Alexander, Leah, d. 3/17/1950, 83y
M.A.
Alexander, Hannah, w/o Thomas
N.A.
Alexander, Naomi, d/o Thomas & Hannah, 12/24/1840-8/2/1876, 35y7m15d
Alexander, Thomas, 3/17/1800-9/2/1871, 71y5m15d
Alexander, Mary, d/o Thomas & Hannah, 11/10/1836-4/7/1871, 34y4m24d
Alexander, James, 9/20/1795-3/14/1865, 69y6m21d
H. A.

Hart, Fred A., 1864-1918
Hart, Bertha M., his wife, 1870-1948
Clark, John R., husband, 1889-1918
Clark, Virginia M., 1890-1960
Cramer, James K., GAR,1847-1922
Cramer, Mathersa H., his wife, mother, 1848-1932
Cramer, Hiram, son, 1876-1877
Erb, Elvin E., 1884-1942
Erb, L. Etta Hart, 1887-1957

Row 9
And__, Mary, d/o Henry & Meigart, d. 11/2/1851, 1y2m18d
Andeus, John Emory, s/o Henry & Meigart, d. 10/20/1851, 5y4m11d
Bascom, Henry, s/o David & Margart Hegan, w: Mary Jane Hagen,
     5/5/1838-10/8/1865, 27y
Hagen, ___, s/o ___ & ___y, can not read small stone
M.A., H.B.H.
Appleton, Harriet, d/o Henry & Sarah, d. 4/6/1849
Cummings, Thos. L., Co. H 122 Pa. Vol., GAR, 2/23/1825-7/6/1905
M.C., A.C.
Carter, Margaret, d. 8/30/1855, 55y5m1d
Carter, Aleander, d. 2/10/1872, 70y11m8d
Campbell, Margaret, w/o John, 1/4/1822-12/24/1911, 89y11m20d
Campbell, John, 7/6/1816-11/19/1895, 79y4m13d
Campbell, Annie E., d/o John & Margt., d. 6/2/1846, 1y3m
Campbell, infant son, d. 1/29/1844
O'Donnel, Maria, 7/16/1811-11/1/1869
R.S.
Douts, Richards W., 1892-1975
Douts, Annie M., w/o Waler, mother, 1898-1918
Neel, Custis D., 1878-1964
Neel, Ida S., his wife, 1879-1940
Armstrong, Christian H., 1853-1923
Armstrong, Henrietta, his wife, 1862-1920
Neel, Jacob M., 1903-1942
Neel, Estella J., his wife, 1903-1973

Row 10
AEC
Spence, Jesse, father, 5/4/1802-11/22/1842
Spence, Rebecca, w/o Jesse, mother, 4/26/1807-3/24/1886
McCombs, Harry, GAR, d. 1/24/1871, 38y
McCombs, John, father, 10/20/1811-6/23/1889, 72y8m3d
McCombs, Rebecca, w/o John, mother, 2/_/1813- broken stone
Fisher, Albert J., GAR, 7/15/1844-8/2/1879, 35y17d

Armstrong, H. Oliver, 1859-1940
Armstrong, Susan E. McMillen, his wife, d/o Martha J., 1864-1937
Armstrong, Martha J., d/o Oliver & Susan, 1892-1895
Armstrong, Jasper B., s/o Oliver & Susan, 1897-1905
C.E.A.
Armstrong, Ralph G., 1884-1956
Armstrong, Barbara A. Stokes, his wife, 1887-1949
Armstrong, F. Myrl, 1909-1919
Armstrong, Paul, Pauline (twins), b/d 1911
Armstrong, Willis S., b/d 1925
Armstrong, Harold R., 1907-1975
Erb, Amos E., 6/18/1876-12/8/1967
Erb, Bertha Sellers, his wife, 4/3/1877-5/5/1922

Row 11
H.M.H.
Koplin, Hiram S., s/o ___ & Margaret, 4/21/1841-4/29/1841
___, ___ in memory of ___, ___/18__, -y-m11d
___ [unable to read these two old stones]

Row 12
J.S.
Shenk, Amoss M., husband, 1897-
Shenk, Ann, wife, 1894-1974
Shenk, Martin G., father, 1866-1902
Shenk, Annie E. Sellers, mother, 1866-1954
Clark, Walter E., 3/2/1875-12/3/1900
Clark, Brice, Pvt. Co. H 79 Pa. Regt., GAR, 4/16/1840-8/_1/1911
Clark, Beatrice, w/o Brice, 1/1/1843-3/15/1917
Shuman, Anna S. Rice, w/o Elmer M. Shuman, 9/14/1873-10/15/1901
Rice, John, Corp'l. Co H 122 Pa. Inf., gov't. stone, no dates
Rice, E. Fred, son, 3/5/1898-3/4/1924
Rice, Maris, s/o Henry & Jennie, 11/2/1902-8/10/1904, 2y9m1d
Rice, W. Henry, 8/7/1864-12/27/1917
Rice, Mary J., 2/4/1867-11/7/1948
Brown, Francis M., 1860-1905
Brown, Mary Emma, his wife, 1864-1945
Warfel, Amos R., 1862-1948
Warfel, Ida M. Sellers, his w., 1872-1941
Warfel, Mabel, 1904-1906
Murry, Amos E., 10/10/1895-12/21/1973
Murry, Esther I., 2/6/903-3/25/1963

Row 13
Campbell, John K., father, 1865-1949

Campbell, Kathyrn C., mother, 1869-1948
Campbell, Authar, 1893-1896
Adams, Ida C., Akens Adams, wife, 10/18/1866-
Akens, George W., husband, 3/25/1853-1/9/1910
Akens, Margaret, mother, 7/10/1820-4/20/1903, 87y9m10d
Akens, Ebenezer, father, 8/25/1810-2/27/1897, 86y6m2d
Erb, Reba, 1/6/1894-11/20/1963
Erb, Henry B., father, 4/10/1853-4/25/1926
Erb, Ida M., 10/29/1851-7/8/1904
Neel, Audley A., b./d. 1898
Neel, Verna E., b,/d. 1902
Neel, Mary Helen, b./d. 190-, ch./o W. R. & Emma L.
Hagen, Kate B., 10/20/1845-1/11/1940
-ell, Aug. C., gov't. stone buried in ground, 1st letter either B, G, D. or O
Murry, Charles E., 1894-1947
Murry, Carrie E. Brown, his wife, 1897-1988
Miller, Leslie J., 1891-1968
Miller, Martha E., 1892-1966
Murry, Myrtle E., 5/21/1894-4/21/1973
Murry, John E., 2/9/1892-
Murry, Minnie E., 1915-1915
Murry, Lester D., b./d. 1929
Wallace, Benjamin J., 1881-1965
Wallace, Minnie E., his wife, 1886-1969
Murry, Amos D., 1853-1923
Murry, Mary L., 1857-1937
Miller, Verna E., mother, 1921-1949
Miller, John L., father, 1914-1985
Miller, James L., 1948-1995. Paul E. 1944-1982

Row 14
Alexander, Charles G., s/o Samuel & Jennie, 10/27/1835-6/9/1909, 23y7m10d
Alexander, Samuel, 1848-1928
Alexander, Jennie M., 1847-1924
Alexander, Chester L., 1871-1954
Murry, George E., 1880-1947
Murry, Daisy E. Shenk, his wife, 1880-1958
Murry, Erma, d/o George & Daisy, b./d. 9/24/1908
Sellers, Chester M., infant, no dates on stone
Jenkins, Roy W., father, 1887-1969
Jenkins, Ida E., mother, 1891-1968
Jenkins, Charles A., s/o Roy & Ida, 11/29-12/4/1911
Alexander, H. Clinton, father, 1879-1953
Alexander, Mabel Brubaker, mother, 1882-1918

Sowers, Conrad, husband, GAR, 1840-1928
Sowers, Amanda C., wife, 1841-1931
Clark, Claude I., s/o Harry E. & Henreitta, 9/6/1881-3/11/1896, 4y6m5d
Clark, Harry E., father, 1860-1917
Clark, Henrietta, his wife, mother, 1860-1938
Farmer, John C., 1882-1935
Farmer, Kathryn E., his wife, 1887-1923
Girvin, Mercer R., M.D., father, 1868-1923
Girvin, Lillian M., mother, 1872-1935
Clark, Ross L., father, 1889-1943
Clark, Mildred V. Kennedy, mother, 1892-1942

Row 15
Hart, Clarence R., father, 1887-1930
Hart, Daisy M. Lehman, mother, his wife, 1886-1977
Moss, James H., 1852-1919
Moss, Annie S., 1862-1942
Alexander, Cloyd G., s/o B. Emerson & Anna L., 1927-1931
Stevenson, S. C., GAR, 1/20/1842-4/10/1933
Stevenson, Mary, 8/25/1842-5/8/1913
Heiney, Samuel, father, 1884-1965
Heiney, Florence M., mother, 1885-1959
Heiney, Harry D., s/o Sam & Flo, 11/17/1912-10/7/1914, 1y10m20d
Campbell, Andrew A., 2/12/1854-2/15/1927
Campbell, Fanny, mother, 11/20/1852-3/18/1915
Campbell, Clara, 12/7/1875-7/26/1954
Campbell, Samuel, 10/29/1848-11/5/1916, 68y5d
Neff, Bessie May, 1887-1937
Neff, Guy W., d/o Bessie, 1913-1918
Neff, Alonzo R., 1883-1977
Sellers, Frank, s/o Wm. & Viola M., 1/30-3/3/1923
Madigan, Edward J., 1856-1929
Campbell, Henry H., 9/30/1862-4/10/1934
Campbell, George, 1902-1953

Row 16
Hart, Wyett W., 1861-1930
Hart, Edith Keller, his wife, 1868-1933
Stokes, Jacob R., father, 1878-1956
Stokes, Suie J., mother, 1881-1961
Hershey, Mary, mother, 8/27/1878-3/21/1963
Hershey, Enos B., 3/28/1871-9/4/1952
Stevenson, George E., 1863-1934
Stevenson, Emma E. Shoff, his wife, 1877-1919
Groff, Daniel, 4/1/1839-9/17/1926

Groff, Margaret M., his wife, 12/21/1848-10/5/1919
Holtzinger, Amos H., 1838-1922
Holtzinger, Mary J. Armstrong, his wife, 1853-
Beach, Ella Nora Erb, 3/31/1876-2/12/1957
Erb, Myrtle L., d/o Elmer E. & Edna E., 2/26-4/20/1928
Erb, Pearl E., d/do Elmer E. & Edna E., 5/5-8/1929
Erb, Lloyd, 1931-2
Erb, Lowell, 1933-34
Erb, Floyd D., 1936-8
Erb, Edna C., 1897-1940
Erb, Elmer E., 1894-1946

Row 17
Herr, Franklin M., 1861-1951
Herr, Rebecca, his wife, 1862-1931
Gerlach, Abram E., 1867-1941
Gerlach, Elizabeth W. Doerstler, his wife, 1866-1952
Shoff, Clinton E., 1/4/1884-5/13/1963
Shoff, Emma D., 9/2/1890-7/29/1973
Shoff, Gerald C., b/d 3/16/1938
Tomlinson, Edgar M., father, 1883-1923
Tomlinson, Ella D., mother, 1893-1975
Erb, S. Columbus, 12/4/1896-4/18/1973
Erb, Ada A., 5/26/1903-
Miles, John H., 9/23/1853-5/1/1928
Miles, Lucilla, 6/7/1857-1/18/1931
Walton, Edward L., father, 1854-1928
Walton, Mary J., mother, 1894-1931
Frymyer, Wm. S., 9/23/1925-8/5/1937

Row 18
Gainer, Clarence C., 1906-1932
Gainer, Mary V. Hackman, his wife, 1904-1952
Adams, Robert H., 7/26/1906-
Adams, C. Marie, 12/26/1910-
Kreider, Lloyd R., 3/22/1904-
Kreider, M. Fern, 5/22/1903-7/8/1978
Cramer, George, 1889-1965
Cramer, Mary Warfel, his wife, 1893-
Cramer, Clara W., d/o George & Mary, 1918-1939
Drumm, John M., 1857-1946
Drumm, Sarah A., 1858-1946
Drumm, Martha, d/o John & Sarah, d. 1894, 9m
Drumm, George, 1882-1961
Drumm, Cora Irene, 1880-1943

Drumm, John R., Lt. Col. Army Air Corp., WWI, 1889-1965
Jefferies, Cora Irene, w/o Thomas B., d/o Sarah & John Drumm, 1880-1943
Douts, John E., 1932-1945
Douts, Charles, 1898-1953
Douts, Ada W. Erb, his wife, 1900-
Bowers, Doris D., 1929-1975

Row 19
Carter, Harold St. Clair, 1895-1971
Carter, Lillian M., 1895-1974
Carter, Harold St. Clair, Jr., 1923-1956
Carter, Doris A., 1924-
Shoff, Annie H., 1889-
Shoff, Benjamin R., 1890-1947
Stevenson, Samuel E., father, 1910
Stevenson, Dorothy E., mother, 1914-1945
Erb, Wm. W., 1863-1949
Erb, Emma D., his wife, 1866-1948

Row 20
Hart, Wm. Clarence, s/o Glenn & Laura, 4/11-15/1949, 4d
___ blank stone
Mark, Robert P., 2/4-7/1947, 3d
Wissler, Chester E., 1905-1978
Jones, Howard E., 9/13/1903-1_/22/1968
Jones, V. Mae, 10/16/1903-

Row 21
Waller, Kenneth Charles J., 1961-1962
Graybill, Raymond H., father, 1896-1972
Graybill, Florence E. Drumm, mother, 1900-1960
Douts, Emerson, 1890-1977
Douts, Mary Walton, his wife, 1894-1963
Gainer, Emory W., 1874-1954
Gainer, A. Blanche Clark, 1878-1958
Gainer, Oleta, 1924-
Gainer, Adam M., 1920-1969

Flory Mill Cemetery

I took the Martic Heights Drive to Hilldale Rd. turning left, going over to Marticville Rd. There at the corner of Hilldale & Marticville Rds. was a single grave on Flory Mill land; Flory, Paul Bowman, son, 1933-1935. It was obvious that there had been more Flory graves here, which had been displaced by Hilldale Road which was cut through this corner of the Mill land.

BETHESDA METHODIST CHURCH CEMETERY
Compiled by Jenne Renkin, Dec. 1978

Ellis & Evans *1883 History of Lancaster County, Pennsylvania*, on page 973, states that "Bethesda is situated in the southwestern part of the township, about 1 mile North of ... McCall's Ferry ... 1 Methodist Church."

Today you take Rt 272 from Lancaster (going down Prince Street) to the Buck, turn right and on Rt. 372 until you are past Muddy Run Park and on the hill to your left is a two-story white church, with a cemetery beside and around it. Turn left on Hilldale Rd.; at the corner of Bethesda Church Road and Hilldale is the church. It is about 2 miles from Rawlinsville and is on the way to Holtwood. This church is 17.5 miles from Lancaster.

Among persons buried here are members of the Mt. Nebo Armstrong clan; including my ancestress, Margaret Armstrong Stewart O'Nail's only daughter, Nancy O'Nail Cully, w/o David Cully.

Row 1
Trimble(?), Eliza, w/o James H., mother, 4/30/1834-12/13/1923
Trimble(?), James H., 6/20/1836-7/7/1915
Mother: Mary Stively
Stively, Thomas, no dates, father, erected by Horace & Frances
Sweigart, Benj. L., 1853-1928
Sweigart, M. Eliz. Clark, his wife, 1854-1920
Sweigart, Mary A., 1876-1967
Sweigart, Theresa M., 1882-1934
Sweigart, John, 1883-1922
Sweigart, Felix C., 1878-1881
Ressler, Clarence E., 8/16/1884-9/10/1943
Ressler, Carrie R. Cramer, his wife, 4/5/1885-5/16/1951
Cramer, Owen, 12/28/1849-4/25/1920
Cramer, Elmira, his wife, 1/31/1844-3/15/1910
Galen, Wm. Henry, 2/22/1849-1/2/1911
Galen, Sarah Elizabeth, wife, 12/29/1851-2/9/1911
Eshleman, S. Clayton, 1867-1934
Eshleman, Maude M., wife, 1872-1964

In front of 1st row
Cramer, Edgar, s/o L. & A., 1/20/1886-3/14/1886, 1m25d

Cramer, Amelia, w/o Lewis (Louis), 1857-1939
Cramer, Louis, husband, 9/16/1847-6/5/1915
Cramer, Walter, 1885-1932
Cramer, Thomas B., 1851-1903
Cramer, Amelia W., wife, 1856-1898
Cramer, Irvin, 10/7/1878-4/22/1961
Cramer, Katie Feiler, wife, 2/11/1882-7/15/1966
Cramer, Gertrude, 12/27/1918-4/14/1979
Eisenberger, Abram, 1856-1941
Eisenberger, Regina, wife, 1854-1908
Eisenberger, Maris, 1854-1927
Eisenberger, Sarah, wife, 1854-1948
Cramer, John M., 1867-1944
Cramer, Ida, his wife, 1875-1935
Wiggins, Frank M., father, 1875-1959
Wiggins, Lillie E., mother, 1880-1956

Shaub, Arthur Z., 4/21/1886-3/3/1951
Shaub, Clara Cramer, wife, 4/3/1887-11/6/1950
Shaub, Ruth E., dau., 11/10/1909-2/18/1915
Moore, Samuel, father, 9/5/1881-10/18/1959
Moore, Sylvia, mother, 3/29/1881-8/17/1914
Clark, John D., father, 1862-1938
Clark, Ella M., mother, 1863-1938
Robinson, Rachel, w/o Isaac, 12/17/1822-1/30/1908
Robinson, Isaac, 12/17/1821-4/7/1906, 84y6m24d
Myers-Clark, Samuel J., 4/20/1880-2/19/1961
Myers-Clark, Bessie G., 3/28/1884-12/28/1939
Myers-Clark, Joseph H., 1/29/1856-12/5/1940
Myers-Clark, Mary A., 4/10/1861-9/27/1946
Stauffer, Hiram, 1849-1942
Stauffer, Fannie M., his wife, 1849-1923

Ecklin, James, 12/25/1818-2/27/1901. Grandfather
M.M.E.
Buchanan, Margaret, w/o John, d/o John & Jane Ecklin, 3/25/18__ -
    4/115/1886, 78y21d. Stone broken (1825)
Ecklin, Martha, d/o Jo. D. & L. A., b/d 1881
Ecklin, David K., s/o Jo. D. & L. A., 8/23/1886-7/15/1889, 2y10m23d
Ecklin, Joseph D., 2/11/1849-2/6/1890, 40y11m28d
Ecklin, Antha Letitia, w/o Joseph D., 1/14/1851-6/4/1918, 67y5m10d
Harner, infant dau., can not read
Harner, Rebecca A., w/o Joseph, 11/17/1839-4/11/1909
Harner, Joseph, 9/24/1832-4/4/1909
Rutter, Harry B., 1/10/1871-2/2/1958

Rutter, Annie Alice Harner, 4/25/1867-10/19/1951
Harner, Jesse, 1/20/1835-12/6/1914
Harner, Mary E., his wife, 11/25/1834-10/4/1885
Dodd, Nora E., 4/30/1871-6/20/1949
Yost, Irma Clare, d/o John F. & Emma P., 7/17/1874-4/25/1889
Yost, Emma Patton, w/o John F., 1/9/1850-12/1/1917
Yost, John F., M.D., 8/4/1841-4/7/1925
Ambler, Harry C., 1874-1933
Ambler, Clara E., 1870-1958
Ambler, Horace O., son, 1897-1898
Harner, J. Wilmer, 1867-1961
Harner, Belle W., wife, 1872-1942
Harner, Frederick, son, 1915-1916
Harner, Marvin, son, Co. I 4th Infantry Division, WWI, 1894-1918

Church

Row 1 continued
Brubaker, George I. 1902
Brubaker, Mary M. 1905
Pollock, Kathryn C., 1902-1978
Pollock, Raymond A., 1898-1955
Bortzfield, June M., 1922-. Frank M., 1918-
Myers, M. Jane, Sept. 1, 1906 - Jan. 27, 1986; Milfred C. Jan. 5, 1907 -
    Jan. 29, 1991
Smith, Ira P., 11/26/1877-2/22/1964
Conrad, Samuel A., Sr., Aug. 4, 1914 - Sept. 18, 1979. Mary E., July 15,
    1922
Dunkle, Erma G., 1897-
Dunkle, Clyde A., 1896-1976
Dunkle, Sue K., 1875-1961
Dunkle, J. Elmer, 1871-1955
Eshleman, Horace M., 1908-1972

Row 5
Moore, Florance R., wife of [below], 1896-1987
Moore, Hartman H., Jr., Batt. D 312 Field Art., 1895-1952
Harner, George E., father, 1869-1918
Nornhold, Emma Harner, mother, 1875-1944
McKinney, Virgie A. Harner, 1897-1988.
Ecklin, Harry W., father, 1876-1967
Ecklin, James F., son, 1901-1976
Ecklin, Cora E., mother, 1878-1938
Ecklin, Mary N., dau., 1907-1908
Dunkle, John O., 1841-1922

Dunkle, Mary Spence, his wife, 1842-1907
Dunkle, Lilian, inf. d/o John & Mary, 4/11-1/1887, 7d
Dunkle, "Ray" Rebecca M., 1879-1945
Wentz, Wm. H., 3/16/1844-12/14/1915
Wentz, Louisa A., 7/15/1851-12/3/1938
Wentz, Walter G., infant son, 1873-1875
McClune, Lindley R., GAR, 3/18/1842-1/3/1892
McClune, Philena Ewing, 6/29/1843-11/25/1914
Erb, Elizabeth K., w/o Benj., 8/20/1842-3/1/1914, 71y6m11d
Erb, Benj. W., 10/11/1839-8/2/1913, 73y9m22d
Erb, Isaiah, s/o Benj. & Eliz., brother, 1/22/1863-6/30/1883, 19y10m8d
Tomlinson, John J., 1865-1949
Tomlinson, Amanda L., his wife, 1870-1948

Row 2
Drumm, George W., 1890-1965
Drumm, Deba C., 1895-1926
Drumm, Elsie S., 1887-19__
Harner, Mary K., 5/26/1902-1/20/1967
Foote, Lawrence A., AEF, WWI, 11/6/1895-5/14/1948
Foote, Alice Harner, wife, 5/26/1902-
Foote, Eleanor Carol, 2/19/1936-
Armstrong, Elsie Clayre, d/o Clarence Wm. & B. Mild., 7/30/1933-
   8/14/1958 *NOTE: Elsie Clayre & Ruthana were killed in KLM airline
   disaster, 8/14/1958.*
Armstrong, B. Mildred Russler, mother, 8/4/1908-
Armstrong, Clarence William, 2/3/1904-6/25/1973
Eckman, Martha Broslet, no dates on stone
Eckman, Elsie J., 4/22/1878-3/1/1950
Armstrong, Ruthana, 5/23/1933-8/14/1958
Armstrong, Anna M., mother, 9/23/1908-6/16/1977
Armstrong, Ralph C., father, 5/9/1901-5/9/1970
Espensade, Annie I., 1881-1976
Espensade, C. Earl, 1900-1969

Row 4
Erb, Joseph B., 7/18/1816-3/7/1895, 78y7m19d
Erb, Magdalena, w/o Joseph B., 5/24/1812-3/16/1885, 72y9m19d
Dunkle, Margaret I., 4/2/1819-12/7/1897, 78y8m5d
Dunkle, George W., 9/10/1818-5/11/1896, 77y8m1d
Dunkle, Willie, inf. s/o J. B. & __, b/d 1873
Dunkle, J. Benton, father, 1844-1922
Dunkle, Marietta, his wife, mother, 1851-1926
Wentz, Paul, s/o E. Roy & Leila E. Eshleman, 5/29-9/8/1906
Wentz, Charles Elvin, 10/14/1876-9/12/1940

Wentz, Viola Webster, wife, 10/15/1876-11/18/1958
Wentz, Susan, d/o Joseph & Sarah, 2/22/1802-12/16/1877
Wentz, John S., 11/20/1805,3/30/1883, 77y1m10d
Wentz, Sarah A. Penny, w/o John S. Wentz, d. 11/17/1873, 59y3m23d
Barclay, John F., 1870-1944
Barclay, Ellie N., wife, 1870-1950
Barclay, Anna Myrtle, dau., 1905-1906
Kinsey, Wm. H., 6/7/1883-12/23/1928
Kinsey, Annie M., w/o Wm. K., mother, 11/13/1850-1/24/1908, 57y2m11d
Kinsey, William, 3/7/1844-1/21/1909, 64y10m
Adams, Bertha M., mother, 1879-1969
Adams, Lawrence C., father, 1877-1959
Myers, Wm. Benj., husband, 1904-1982
Myers, Anna Adams, wife, 1907-1971

Armstrong, William H., father, 1873-1945
Armstrong, E. Marion, mother, 1874-1922
Brimmer, Blanche C., 1890-1961
Brimmer, Lloyd S., 1889-1963
Brimmer, Amie Marguerite, d/o Lloyd & Blanche, 1908-1926
Bard, Lester B., 7/27/1895-1/15/19671
Harnish, Minnie Sieple, 9/17/1905-7/20/1927
Campbell, Laura E., mother, 1890-1953
Campbell, Emmett A., father, 1891-1942
Kauffman, Mary S., 1897-1977
Transue, Grace Kauffman, wife, 9/6/1896-
Transue, Edwin Allen, 10/2/1902-11/18/1965

Row 5 A
___, Leo, Co. ___ 5th Pa.
E.E.K., 3 stone unmarked post
Patton, Mary, 12/10/1785-3/23/1869, 83y3m13d
Snavely, Ellen J., w/o John, 10/18/1814-12/22/1883, 69y2m11d
Snavely, John, 8/8/1819-1/5/1902, 82y-m28d
Seiple, John L., 1895-1902
Seiple, Paul I., 1842-1903, children of L. R. & E. L.
Seiple, Ida M., d/o L. R. & E. L., 8/_9/1903-3/2/1913
Seiple, Joseph, s/o L. R. & E. L., 4/5/1894-7/2/1916
Seiple, Lindley R., 1860-1945
Seiple, Elizabeth E., 1865-1938
Marion, Ida Lou, w/o Edmond, 2/4/1856-10/21/1954
A.G.
Myers, Helen P. Moss, 1922, w/o William B. Myers
Lowy, Karl, s/o Hugo & Sadie M., no year, month or day of death,
    7y8m13d

Bard, J. Martin, 1857-1924
Bard, Ina D., 1863-1941
Bard, Charles W., U.S. Navy WWII, 5/19/1898-3/12/1942
Feiler, Sarah E., 1892-
Feiler, Henry P., 1884-1960
Feiler, Rita Jean, d/o Sarah & Henry, b/d 1933
Feiler, Sara M., d/o Sarah & Henry, 1924-1927
Eshleman, B. Franklin, father, 1897-1956
Eshleman, Jane G., mother, 1894-1937
Eshleman, infant, no date
Immel, Isaac M., father, 1883-1962
Immel, Barbara E., 1888-1928
Kauffman, Edward M., 10/13/1864-4/26/1944
Kauffman, Rhoda N. Sechrist, 8/10/1859-11/6/1932
Kauffman, Thelma Mae, d/o Earl & Clara, 5/6-10/6/1928
Kauffman, Clare Sieple, mother, 1898-1963
Kauffman, Earl S., father, 1894-1965
Kauffman, Edna K. Hickey, 1889-1958

Row 8
McCardle, Eli, Co. D 22nd Pa. Inf., GAR, govt. stone
McCardle, Anna, w/o Samuel, 1851-1925
McCardle, Samuel, Co. D, 195th Pa. Vol., 3/3/1848-3/30/1913
S.
Groff, Samuel, s/o F. & M., b/d 11/8/1853
Groff, Clara Marinda, c/o F. B. & Maria, 10/12/1858-9/8/1859
Groff, Francis B., 3/17/1829-9/8/1884, 55y5m21d
Stone blank
Snodgrass, Margaret, stone broken in 1/4 top 1/2 reset, d. 2/9/1851, 63y
I.D.
Cramer, Elmer, brother, 1893-1972
Drumm, Ida J., 1898-1970
Drumm, Verna M., 1898-1973
Kauffman, I. James, s/o Warren & Anna J., 2/25/1919-9/30/1972
Kauffman, Jay Warren, CPL US Marine Corps, WWII, June 20, 1924-Dec.
    22, 1992

Row 9
Cully, David E., 1855-1914
Cully, Nancy, w/o David, mother, O'Neil, 11/15/1815-9/27/1882,
    66y10m12d
Cully, Margaret Ann, w/o David, 10/18/1826-10/11/1857, 31y15d
Cully, David, 5/1/1818-8/17/1881, __y5m16d
Barclay, Adaline M., 11/10/1829-7/15/1906
Barclay, James F., s/o John B. & Mary, 2/17/1833-6/11/1859

Barclay, Mary, w/o John B., 3/13/1793-7/16/1859
Barclay, John, d. 11/16/1851, 50y
Labezius, George W., 9/16/1816-8/26/1859
two stones blank
Collins, Wm., 9/17/1790-9/28/1853
Collins, Elizabeth M., 11/27/1785-9/21/1866
Labezius, Mary Ann, w/o Thomas, 11/6/18212-4/9/1871
Labezius, Willie, s/o Thomas & Mary A., 7/_/1862-9/13/1865
Labezius, Thomas J., 5/22/1823-11/5/1914
Labezius, Myrl S., s/o Harry & Ella N., 1/5/1896-12/27/1906, 10y11m22d
Labezius, Isabella I., daughter, 11/8/1914-4/10/1932
Labezius, Harry, 8/16/1866-11/15/1947
Labezius, Ella Nora, his wife, 10/15/1875-7/6/1952
E. E., two posts with "E" on them.

Section B
Drumm, Samuel G., father, 1865-1952
Drumm, Anna M., mother, 1863-1939
Drumm, S. Harold, son, 1903-1915

Row 8
Dunkle, Mary Alice Shoemaker, 1865-1945
Dunkle, B. Cookman, 1875-1970
Family head stone: Martin. Father. Ellis J. March 4, 1910, Dec. 4, 1983.
    Mother. Elizabeth S., Aug. 30, 1912
Martin, Nancy Jane, d/o Ellis & Eliz. I., d. 1/21/1934
Barclay, Allison, father, 1894-1942
Barclay, Robert A., PFC, US Army, April 30, 1921, Nov. 24, 1981. Son
Barclay, Helen Shaub, mother, 1896-1954
Patton, Nellie I., 10/10/1877-9/15/1938

Row 9
Patton, John M., 12/17/1870-6/24/1955
White, Margaret A., mother, 1874-1949
White, James, Co. K, 3d US Cav. 1899-1902, 1871-1942
Shaub, Ross Aldus, May 13, 1917, Nov. 24, 1986. Betty Farmer, Sept. 21,
    1918.
Feiler, Dennis, s/o Glenn & Daisy, 5/30/1952-1/22/1954. Feiler, Glenn B.,
    1921-1984. WWII. Daisy Frey, 1924
Erb, Arlene K., Nov. 12, 1912, Feb. 15, 1994. Walter S., Aug. 4, 1908

Row 10
Patton, George McClellan, s/o G. C. & Mary A., 3/2/1865-5/16/1895, 30y
Patton, Mary A., w/o George C., d. 10/31/1893, 60y
Patton, George C., d. 9/16/1890, 65y

Patton, James H., s/o G. C. & M. A., 3/23-4/23/1864, 1m
Patton, Maris W., s/o G. C. & M. A., 1/2/1875-12/27/1879, 4y11m25d
Wentz, Violetta, 2/18/1852-1/13/1924
Wentz, Mary J., 11/2/1824-1/19/1906
Wentz, Thomas, 7/15/1820-6/4/1912
Wentz, Winfield S., d. 11/10/1863, 4y4m17d
___, Adelaide, d/o ___
Wentz, Hariet P., d/o ___, d. 7/22/1847, 2m10d
Wentz, Marinda H., d/o ___
H.
Patton, James, 10/17/1816-8/26/1852
Huss, Anna May, d/o V. M. & Mary L. , 2/11-5/4/1899
Stauffer, Ralph E., 5/26/1887-3/25/1940
Stauffer, Lelia K., his wife, 3/14/1889-3/14/1971

Brubaker, Asa E., father, 3/7/1864-10/20/1952
Brubaker, Flora L., mother, 5/14/1866-9/1/1961
Brubaker, G. Reed, s/o Asa & Flora, 1907-1919
Brubaker, Clarence D., s/o Asa & Flora, 1898-19__
Null, Amos B., father, 7/4/1854-8/14/1915
Null, J. Kenneth, 12/28/1891-10/13/1908

Graybill, Mary E., mother, June 29, 1900 - June 10, 1981
Graybill, Charles P., 10/28/1847-9/2/1953
Harner, Edna M. Barclay, 8/17/1897-1900
Harner, John C., 9/9/1895-1/20/1972
Hershock, Benny Maris, 11/26-11/30/1944
Shaub, Mae Elizabeth, Nov. 28, 1918
Shaub, Marian S., mother, 1895-1967
Shaub, Clarence A., father, 1889-1954
Shaub, infant s/o Marian & Clarence, b/d 9/1/1932
Shaub, Benj. C., Sgt., Co. F 502nd Para. Inf. 101st Div., d. in Holland,
    10/11/1921-11/7/1944
Stevenson, Nancy E., b/d 7/2/1950. Stevenson: Mother. Martha E., Aug.
    16, 1912. Father. William F., Aug. 23, 1912, Dec. 31, 1980
Erb, Cora A., 5/15/1880-11/15/1956
Erb, Maris E., 11/22/1872-9/29/1955

Row 11
C.D.
M.L.D.
Hambleton, Mary E., d. 10/20/1901, 61y1m1d
McLaughlin, Margaret, sister, 9/4.1816-11/18/1891, 75y2m14d
McLaughlin, John, brother, 12/4/1820-11/18/1888, 67y1m14d
McLaughlin, Jennet, mother, d. 4/26/1873, 83y5m6d

McLaughlin, Margaret A. Hambleton, w/o Wm., 1/1/1832-9/20/1918
McLaughlin, William, husband, 10/4/1813-5/1/1893, 69y6m27d
McLaughlin, Mary S., w/o Wm., 10/2/1819-10/27/1879, 60y25d
McLaughlin, Jane, d. 5/15/1868, 68y11m15d
Pennell, Elizabeth, mother, 7/17/1780-10/18/1864, 84y3m1d
Pennell, James T., 4/12/1809-7/28/1879, 70y3m11d
Pennell, Elizabeth, w/o James T., 8/30/1834-3/10/1905
Pennell, Samuel J., 12/7/1870-4/20/1947
Smith, Charles R., s/o Clarkson & Margt. A., Oct.-Dec. 1889
Smith, Wilmer G., 9/4/1882-7/10/1963
Smith, Margaret A., 7/13/1856-11/16/1932
Smith, Clarkson, 7/25/1851-10/3/1920
A post

Kleinhans, Mary, 1822-1896, erected by her son: CH. Handel, 1822-1896
Kleinhuns, "U," A., Co. H 119 Pa. Inf., govt. stone, no date
Brubaker, George W., 2/25/1825-3/30/1907
Brubaker, Esther Ann, his wife, 10/12/1893-8/19/1912
E.B.
Brubaker, Emanuel, son, 1882-1962
Brubaker, Annie E., mother, 1856-1936
Stively, Frank, s/o Lewis & Myrtle, b./d. 10/8/1910
Stively, Myrtle S., w/o Lewis, 2/14/1880-10/29/1906, 26y8m16d

Brubaker, Lena Dorsey, 5/19/1898-1 Apl. 1979
Brubaker, Elmer E., 2/14/1889-3/13/1971
Brubaker, Clara E., 1897-1938
Brubaker: Father - Herbert L. 1894 - 1987. Wife - E. Elmira, 1905-1991
Sellers, Hazel B., 1918-1950
Sellers, James, 1915-
Sellers, baby, no dates
Sinclair, Joseph E., 12/29/1922-
Sinclair, Betty Jane Graybill, wife, 11/13/1924-6/18/1978
Sinclair, James C., 1880-1946
Sinclair, Mary M., 1888-1987
Erb, Ethel M., 1913-
Erb, Maris S., 1910-1964
Brubaker, William, 1869-1939
Brubaker, Delia, 1896-1971
Brubaker, Lottie W., 1878-1957

Row 12
Armstrong, S. Gordon, s/o Hugh 1779-1867, 6/29/1831-12/21/1909, 78y5m22d
Armstrong, Barbara A., 8/26/1832-3/12/1892, 59y6m16d

Armstrong, Josephine, 7/23/1856-2/27/1857, 7m4d
Brown, Fanny, w/o James, d. 2/6/1877, 75y
Clark, Mary Ann, w/o John, 1/25/1827-2/11/1871, 44y17d
Clark, John, father, 5/18/1821-4/12/1904, 82y10m24d
Clark, Amos, s/o John & Mary A., 3/11/1864-10/19/1867, 2y8m8d
Clark, Clarissa, d/o John & Mary A., 2/14/1858-10/8/1866, 8y7m24d
Clark, Emma, d/o John & Mary A., 2/11/1860-9/25/1866, 6y7m13d
Broken stone
Slate stone; stone with German script "G" on it; there are 5 in this row
C. S.
"G"
Clark, sisters, Leonora 1867-1929, Elmyra J. 1851-19__
H, post with H on it
"G" three in a row
Huss, David, 8/1/1818-4/30/1895, 76y9m
Huss, Margaret A., w/o David Huss, 9/25/1820-7/21/1881, 66y9m28d
Huss, Clara M., 3/12/1871-10/15/1878
Huss, Lawrence C., 10/21/1876-10/22/1878, 2y
Huss, Alinede, d/o A. & J. O., 3/_8/6/1875, 5m
Huss, D. Deaver, s/o A. & J. O., 12/_/1879-3/__/1905, 26y6m26d
Huss, Lena A., d/o A. & J. O., 2/14/1880-5/18/1900, 20y3m4d
Huss, Annie A., w/o James O., mother, 6/4/1849-6/14/1925
Huss, James O., father, 7/3/1841-1/24/1896, 51y6m21d
A.
H.
Armstrong, Daniel, 1851-1909
Armstrong, Clara, his wife, 1853-1915,
Armstrong, Myrtle, 1874-1876
1878 Aug. B. Jefferies 1909 (on same stone with Armstrongs)

Alexander, Calvin, 1856-1893
Alexander, Adeline, 1861-1934
Eckman, Ralph, s/o Emmanl. G. & Sallie E., 3/21-7/24/1891, 4m
Eberle, Henry F., father, 1866-1936
Eberle, Lona, mother, 1867-1940
Brubaker, Wm. H., Co. E 2nd Regt. Pa. Cav., 10/28/1837-9/7/1909
Brubaker, Adaline, 5/15/1845-5/24/1924
Bard, John R., 1884-1951
Bard, Esther P., 1889-1947
Bard, Howard C., s/o John R. & Esther P., 3/3-20/1918
Biddle, Ethel M., d/o John R. & Esther P. Bard, 5/7/1909-3/19/1974

Alexander, George C., 1886-1963
Alexander, Suie E., wife, 1885-1965
Alexander, Arthur S., son, 1908-

Alexander, Robert C., son, 1925
Brubaker, Fannie J., 10/11/1907-9/30/1952
Brubaker, Harry T., 8/4/1904-
Brubaker, Goldie V., 1886-1953
Brubaker, Arthur C., 1887-1956
Brubaker, Cletus E., son, 1920-1969
Brubaker, Bertram E., 1908-1974
Brubaker, Marie R., 1912-1964
Brubaker, Bertram E., 1908-1974
Trimble, Ruth Cramer, 1/11/1903-
Trimble, W. Lester, 8/13/1900-
Mundorf, Wm. B., 1900-1977
Mundorf, Pauline, wife, 1904-1972
Mundorf, Sarah E., mother, 1870-1938

Row 13
J. Oldham, there are four (4) stone posts in a row with this on top of
   them
Cramer, Adalaide, w/o Hiram Isenberger, 7/15/1858-9/28/1878, 20y2m18d
Cramer, Samuel, 12/5/1815-8/1/1885, 69y7m30d
Cramer, Susanna, w/o Samuel, 6/19/1823-11/26/1862, 39y5m7d
Cramer, Margaret A., sister, 1856-1921
Cramer, Mary E., w/o Jacob Foltz, 10/16/1845-8/20/1918
Cramer, John Henry, s/o David & Eliz., 3/20/1843-1/1/1855, 6y9m18d
Cramer, David, 7/2/1813-10/_/1883, 41y3m-3d
Cramer, Elizabeth, w/o David, 6/28/1812-10/7/1883, 71y3m9d
Cramer, Mary Ann, w/o John, 12/22/1783-7/9/1844, 60y6m17d
Cramer, John, 11/6/1784-5/18/1848
Cramer, John, brother, d. 12/26/1900, 75y2m13d
Creamer, Susan, w/o Amos Walton, 10/27/1822-10/17/1905
Bellamy, Samuel, s/o Charles & Sus__, 12/31/1847-7/11/1850, 2y7m8d
Bellamy, Susanna, w/o George, d. 10/12/1856, about 70y
Bellamy, George, d. 3/1/1863, 81y
S. C.
Nelson, infant
Nelson, Viola
Nelson, Thomas
Nelson, Stephen F., father, 1845-1921
Nelson, Mary J., mother, 1857-1900
Nelson, Wm. H., 1889-1910
N. J. B., two stone posts, one with "N" one with "J.B."

Barclay, Selinda, mother, d. 7/6/1921
Barclay, John R., father, 3/12/1836-1/28/1909, 72y10m16d
Barclay, Infant dau./Charles & Eva J., b./d. Aug 8, 1888

Barclay, Infant dau./Charles & Eva J., b/d. 3/11/1894
Barclay, Charles S., 1858-1931
Barclay, Eva J., his wife, 1863-1940
Nelson, John C., 1844-1901
Nelson, Isabella Shoff, his wife, 1843-1914
Nelson, Stephen R., son, 1867-1956
Nelson, L. Jennie N. Anstat, daughter, 1870-1898

Rae, John H., 1888-1938
Rae, Esther J., 1899-19__
Miles, Helen M., 6/3/1901-3/30/1964
Miles, John E., 7/7/1899-3/18/1976
Adams, Richard E., 11/13/1848-2/9/1971
Adams, Lester R., 9/25/1905-9/2/1967
Adams, Verna M. Kirk, wife, 3/3/1917-
Quade, Frederick J., 1880-1934
Quade, Cora Null, wife, 1879-1949
Quade, Carl C., 1905-1978
Feiler, Regie, 6/29/1883-9/19/1971
Hamil, Clayton W., 1873-1927
Hamil, Mary M., 1878-1957

Row 14
Null, M. Edna ABT, 5/1/1897-7/7/1967
Null, Martha, 3/10/1855-7/31/1917
Null, Lawrence W., s/o Emory & Martha, d. 7/25/1889, 2y7m8d
Null, Emory T., Co. D 2nd Rgt. Pa. Cav., 11/7/1848-11/28/1927
Null, Isaac W., father, 7/20/1821-1/6/1897, 76y
Null, Elizabeth, w/o Isaac W., d. 6/6/1896, 72y
Null, Franklin A., 4/22/1857-12/10/1862, 5y6m19d
Null, Joseph, s/o Isaac & Eliz. J., J_/11/1851/3/l19/1851
Eckman, infant son, s/o of Hiram & Sarah, d. 3/7/1859
Eckman, George H., s/o Hiram & Sarah, 6/27/1861-9/14/1866, 5y2m17d
Eckman, infant son, s/o of Hiram & Sarah, 8/10-9/18/1866
Eckman, Mary M., d/o Hiram & Sarah, 5/7/1864-9/26/1866, 2y4m19d
Eckman, Ralph, s/o Lizzie, 4/1881-8/1882, 1y4m
Hammond, Thomas F., s/o Wm. & Ann, d. 1850, 19y
W.F.
Ferguson, Wm., d. 7/11/1845, 51y8m18d
4 broken stones
Seiple, Bessie N., 3/20-4/1/1895
Seiple, Verna M., 1898-1901
Seiple, Luella R., d/o W. H. & M. A., 4/26/1900-10/24/1906
Seiple, Wm. H., 1852-1938
Seiple, Mary A., 1858-1920

Kinsey, Henry H., father, 1849-1940
Kinsey, Almira E., mother, 1853-1891
H.P.W. W.S.W.
Shoff, Felix, Co. D Ind. P.T. Pa. L.A., 1848-1901
Shoff, Mary M. Eckman, his wife, 1866-1895
Feiler, John, 1847-1917
Feiler, Dorothea, 1848-1933
Feiler, infant s/o John C. & Amalia, d. 1921

Feiler, Mollie, 1887-
Feiler, John G., WWI, 1888-1969
Greis, Christian, 12/26/1864-5/21/1958
Wells, Amemia, w/o Ward E., d. 1/25/1926
Kauffman, Leviere H., son, 1892-1970
Kauffman, Isaac G., 9/4/1868-6/12/1947
Kauffman, Lizzie S., wife, 9/23/1866-12/27/1927
Oldham, Dora E., 6/16/1908-9/21/1931
Oldham, Ethel H., 1911-1976
Oldham, Elmer H., 1906-1966
Oldham, Harry T., 1886-1951
Stauffer, Elizabeth, 11/23/1888-5/29/1952
Stauffer, Henry, 3/20/1882-8/18/1953
Herr, Lettie S., 8/14/1891-5/27/1965
Herr, Amos F., 3/23/1893-4/28/1967
Herr, John, 1887-1937
Herr, Myrtle, 1889-1965

Row 15
J. Mc.L., foot stone
- Mc. L., foot stone
M.H.
2 small broken stones
W.
small stone
S.W.
C.D.P.
White, Charles, 12/20/1833-12/28/1857, 24y8d
Eckman, Hiram, father, 1834-1897
Eckman, Sarah M., his wife, mother, 1835-1926
M.S.
G. [stone with German script type letter on it, looks like a fancy "G"]
M.S.S.
H.E.K.
Kinsey, Shad. B., Co. K 1 Pa. Vol., govt. stone, GAR marker, d. 1919

___, Hannah E., s/o M. H. ___ [unable to read]
J.H.B., A. W. (posts)
Bechtold, infant s/ M. & E. J., can not read
Bechtold, s/o M. & E. J., can not read
Bechtold, Addison, s/o M. & E. J., age
Bechtold, Evan J., 1869-1938
Bechtold, Mary A., his wife, 1873-1943
Cramer, Wm. M., s/o Wm. H. & Mary E., 5/6/1909-1/20/1910
Cramer, Wm. H., 1878-1957
Cramer, Effie, his wife, 1882-1953
Cramer, infant, dd. 1910
Cramer, Mary E., 12/17/1881-4/15/1910
E.P.

Kauffman, Hobert C., s/o Hobert G. & Myrtle, 8/8/1923-6/18/1935
Kauffman, Myrtle H., 12/27/1902-12/30/1942
Kauffman, Hobert G., 12/14/1896-10/22/1973
Cover, Daily S., 1881-1954
Cover, Grace E., w/o Raymond, mother, 1905-1940
Boon, Pete, 1904-
Boon, Viola R. Graver, 1907-1977
Boon, Carl L., s/o Peter & Viola, 6/28/1930-10/4/1947
Ainsworth, Harriet Deen, infant, 6/4-5/1936
A I S A G, posts

Row 16
Broken stone
G.W.L., foot stone
J.F.B., foot stone
Small worn stone
A.G.I., foot stone
Isenberger, Henry, father, 10/3/1824-1/5/1870
Isenberger, Rosana, mother, 1/18/1830-12/7/1910
Isenberger, Francis E., son, 7/21/1863-4/7/1926
Child's stone, can not read
Broken stone
Eckman, Mahlon P., father, 1831-1902
Eckman, Margaret J., mother, 1834-1907
Eckman, John, son, d.___, 1y6m
Eckman, Susan, 1829-1899
Walton, Elmer A., 1869-1944
Walton, Harriet J. Appleton, wife, 1871-1954
Appleton, Louella A., her sister, 1866-1954

Appleton, John B., father, 1834-1871
Appleton, Mary S., mother, 1831-1919
Ban, James, 3 small stones, no dates
Ban, infant
Ban, Mary
Oldham, Jas. P., Co C 5th Pa. Art., GAR marker, gov't. stone, d. 1925
Oldham, Charles W., USMC, WWI, 4/6/1892-1/21/1957
Funk, Dorothy M., d/o Thomas & Eliz., 2/6/1900-9/13/1906

Oldham, H___, broken gov't. stone, can only read name
Grimsey, Clara E., d/o Charles G. & Grace A., 12/3/1917-1/18/1919
Grimsey, Elizabeth A., d/o Charles G. & Grace A., b./d. 5/5/1913
Grimsey, William H., s/o Charles G. & Grace A., 12/16/1933-1/11/1934
Grimsey, Grace A., 2/26/1890-3/9/1970
Grimsey, Charles G., 9/12/1885-10/8/1965
Null, Walter P., 8/26/1883-1/10/1961
Null, Susan W., 4/6/1889-8/3/1927
Labezius, Russel H., s/o R. H. & Eliz. F., 8/9-10/22-1929
Labezius, Robert Donald, s/o Russel H. & Eliz. F. Miller, Korean War,
    9/24/1933-7/1/1975
Cramer, Josetta F., s/o Harold & Helen, 6/30-12/7/1933
Cramer, Helen M., 1912-
Cramer, Harold J., 1912-1959
Ballantyne, Wm. M. H., 1886-1949
Ballantyne, Jessie L., 1867-1950
Ballantyne, Jean McLennan, born Aberdeen, Scotland, 6/8/1890-
    10/12/1970
Wells, Ward E., 10/14/1884-9/27/1963
Wells, Clare Ballantyne, wife, 1/16/1884-1/7/1943
Ballantyne, James, 1854-1935
Ballantyne, Elizabeth Jardine, wife, 1928-

Row 17
Nelson, Isabel, 1843-1914
Nelson, John, 1849-1901
Fisher, Jno., Corpl. Co. K 7th Pa. Cav., Gov't. stone
Holbein, Emma, d/o Harry & Lucie, 12/8/1907-Jun/ 8/1917
Thompson, Harry, 8/26/1858-12/22/1885, 27y3m26d

Field stone
Stephens, T. M., Co. K 5th Md. Inf., 1910
Kauffman, Warren S., 7/16/1889-3/23/1977
Kauffman, Anna J. Wickersham, wife, 3/8/1886-11/12/1934
Kauffman, Kathryn M., 1912-1916
Alexander, Bessie M., 1891-

Alexander, Chester J., 1885-1967

A.
N.
E.G.
Urban, W. Victor, s/o Guy K. & Edna K., 1918-1927
Urban, Dorothy M., d/o Guy K. & Edna K., 1917-1927
Urban, Guy K., 7/24/1892-5/22/1960
Urban, Edna Douglas, 10/25/1894-6/24/1974
McLune, I. Paul, brother, WWI, 1893-1961
McLune, A. Myrtle, sister, 1898-1974
Stauffer, Samuel, 1893-1956
Stauffer, Frank, 1887-1960
Peterson, Andy, 1872-1954
R.R.

Row 18
Ambler, I. Lucile Hendricks, 5/23/1908-
Ambler, Thomas E., 8/8/1910-
Doss, A. Elizabeth Hendricks, 4/5/1915-11/26/1966
Graver, Shaun Douglas, son, 7/7-18/1969
Abbot, James, 1945-1969
Quade, Elmer H., WWI, 5/18/1894-11/3/1977
Graver, Mary W., 10/30/1918-8/17/1978
Graver, Chester H., 11/2/1918-
Shenk, Lee M., 7/9/1916-
Shenk, Helen K., 8/1/1917-5/21/1978
Boyd, Reba Snyder, 1929-1977
Boyd, Clifford C., 1924-
Stevenson, Wm. E., 9/15/1944-
Stevenson, Joan P., 3/4/1945-6/3/1974
Pennington, Troy Michael, son, 5/10/1972-4/11/1977

RAWLINSVILLE METHODIST CHURCH CEMETERY
Compiled by Jenne Renkin, April 1978

Row 1
Hagen
Herr, Emma F., 1887-1972
Herr, Harry H., 1890-1940
Herr, Harry H., Jr., s/o Emma F. & Harry H., 1928-1931
Armstrong, Daniel O., 1869-1964
Armstrong, Hattie S., wife, 1884-1920
Armstrong, James N., child, 1917-1919

Armstrong, Howard H., child, 1919-1919
Cramer, Lawrence C., 1884-1956
Cramer, Gertrude, wife, 1887-1925
Cramer, Betty, daughter, 1923-1923
Leigh, Dora Cramer, 1882-1974
Leigh, John C., 1873-1940
Leigh, Lester W., son, 1909-1937
Cramer, Rose, 8/10/1880-1/24/1958
Galen, John, 1841-1924
Galen, Kate, 1844-1920

Row 2
Mellegan, Olive, 1881-1967
Cramer, John C., Co. B 7 Rgt. PV Cav., 1846-1935
Cramer, Catharine, wife, 1852-1934
Cramer, Maurice, son, 1882-1964
Cramer, David, 2/20/1833-8/1/1904, 71y5m11d
___, Calvin A., son, 8/_/188- -11/22/188-, Cramer?
Reese, Maris, 1857-1927
Reese, Jennie, wife, 1858-1896
Reese, Olice C., s/o Maris & Jennie, 8/24/1881-11/22/1889, 8y2m23d
Hart, Samuel, 1856-1917
Hart, Lizzie H., 1862-1916
Hart, Benjamin, s/o Henry & Eliz., 3/27/1852-2/2/1926
Cramer, Joseph, 1872-1959
Cramer, Mary E. Douts, wife, 1881-1968
Cramer, Walter, son, 7/4/1912-8/5/1913
Cramer, Mary, daughter, 12/20/1904-7/22/1913
Trissler, David T., 1862-1936
Trissler, Sarah, wife, 1859-1953
Trissler, Mabel M., daughter, 1887-1918
Cramer, Daniel C. Jr., 1878-1943
Cramer, Orella M., 1883-1936
Frownfelter, Wm. C., t/sgt/035 bomb qrp, WWII, 10/8/1923-3/3/1971
Heeps, Helen E., 1919-1977
Heeps, Wm. H. Jr., 69th Div. WWII, 1917-

Row 3
Monteith, Chester L., s/o Levi H. & Martha W., 1873-1933
Monteith, Dora G., 1875-1951
Monteith, John, 1818-1909
Monteith, Dailah, 1810-1884
Monteith, William H., s/o John & Delilah, 6/5/1841-3/5/1876, 31y9m
Monteith, Martha W., w/o Levi H., 11/18/1849-12/19/1878, 28y1m1d
Monteith, Levi H., 1841-1920

Monteith, John D., s/o Levi & Martha, 8/_/1878-12/8/1879, 1y4m
Walton, William A., son, 3/27/1872-3/23/1943
Walton, M. Della, d/o Mahlon & Annie, 5/9/1890-4/2/1927
Walton, Bertha D., sister, d/o Mahlon & Annie, 8/22/1869-11/27/1908
Walton, Mahlon Y., 1828-1896
Walton, Annie E., 1839-1922
Walton, John M., 9/15/1862-2/21/1894
Rhoads, Jacob, Co. K 10 Regt. Pa. Vol. Inf., gov't. stone, GAR, d. 1918
Rhoads, Mary C., 1856-1926
Smith, David, 2/29-1840-4/15/1901
Smith, Mary Emma, 6/6/1843-8/11/1931
Smith, Martha M., d/o David & Mary, d. 6/25/1878, 16y10m22d
Smith, Justus Rea, 9/26/1881-3/26/1899
Stokes, Willis Earl, 1888-1948
Stokes, Ida Duffy, wife, 1889-1968
Smith, Maria, w/o Joseph, 10/5/1817-1/20/1907, 89y6m17d
Smith, Joseph, 1/_/18-9 - 1883, 69y
Kuhns, Sarah C., w/o John, 1837-2/17/1895, 58y
Kuhns, John, Co. O 91st Mass. Inf., gov't. stone, GAR, d. 1909
Handel, Frances (Francis?) L., s/o Charles H. & Mary M., 11/29/1898-
    12/_/1898, 1m
Handel, John M., s/o Charles H. & Mary M., 12/13/1876-2/21/1898, 18y
Handel, Charles H., 10/15/1849-7/13/1926
Handel, Mary M., w/o Charles, 2/7/1848-12/26/1937
Handel, William A., 12/8/1882-4/29/1956
Mueller, G. Michael, 2/12/1863-11/29/1938
Mueller, L. Christine Spahr, w/o G. Michael, 5/9/1863-3/2/1898
Adams, Maria G., 1847-1917
Adams, A. J., 1847-1928
Adams, Jacob C., s/o A. J. & Maria G., 10/28/1884-11/24/1906, 21y4m28d
Alexander, William H. P., son, US Navy, WWII, 6/9,1918-1/15/1972
Alexander, Susan F., mother, 2/2/1889-
Alexander, T. Edward, father, 7/16/1892-12/12/1918
Alexander, George E., son, 4/23/1913-2/29/1960
Heeps, Anna May, 1878-1950
Heeps, Wm. H., confirmed by US Senate 1921, 1868-1945
Dickson, Hazel Heeps, 1906-1967
Alexander, Lloyd E., 1883-1957
Alexander, Orella R., w/o Lloyd E., 1888-
Alexander, Erma B., daughter, 1911-1968

Row 4
Witmer, Arthur, 6/3/1875-6/17/1876, 1y12d
Silverthorn, Ella Todd, 1861-1945
Silverthorn, Aaron, 9/12/1860-3/25/1906

Wilson, Josiah Jeffers, s/o Josh & Rachel Wilson, 9/26/1850-7/5/1876, 26y9m9d
Fehl, Eliza J., nee Wilson, 6/16/1852-9/5/1909
Morrison, Ella M., in the __yr. of her age
Moore, Samuel, 8/19/1802-7/2/1890, 87y10m14d
Moore, Mary, 11/1/18__ - 9/1/1887, 71y10m
Moore, M.M.
Moore, Samuel, Co. D 122 Pl., gov't. stone, GAR, d. 1893
Silverthorn, Mary U., d/o Hiram, 11/29/18-__/ 9/9/1902, 52y9m1d
Silverthorn, Clinton, s/o Hiram & S. E., 1/11/1877-9/19/1877
Silverthorn, Sarah E., w/o Hiram, 1/16/1855-11/29/1878, -9y8m3d
Silverthorn, Hiram, 10/25/1842-11/27/1920, 78y1m4d
Silverthorn, Samuel, 12/16/1815-3/23/1879, 63y3m7d
Silverthorn, Martha, w/o Samuel, 10/7/1821-4/16/1900, 78y6m9d
Silverthorn, Catharine, d/o Samuel & Martha, 1/9/1855-12/5/1884, 29y10m27d
Sullivan, James A., 11/10/1838-1/15/1886, 47y-m25d
Sullivan, Eliza A., wife, 5/23/1848-7/19/188_, _8y_m17d
Sullivan, Katie E., dau., 8/29/1877-11/16/1877, 4m17d
Miller, John W., 9/20/1851-11/11/1938
Miller, Clara L., wife, 12/22/1854-7/4/1900
Kilburn, Blanche O., no stone, funeral marker, 1/1/1888-11/5/1964
Miller, Harry D., 9/15/1879-2/29/1912
Kreider, Sarah A., w/o B. F. Kreider, mother, 4/9/1845-11/30/1906, 61y-m2d
Handel, Ruth K., 1894-1918
Mueller, Catherine C., sister, 12/14/1887_8/5/1966
Mueller, Rosa L., sister, 1/27/1890-
Farmer, Minnie M., 1884-1961
Farmer, Harry H., 1878-1957
Moore, Carrie W., 2/21/1869-10/8/1953
Moore, John T., 9/22/1865-12/30/1940
Rhoades, Viola M., no stone, funeral marker, 1897-1978
Erb, Martha E., 1907-
Erb, Albert A., 1904-1971

Row 5
W.A.F.
__, P., stone broken, 1900-1902
Graman, Francina, 4/21/1828-6/15/1901
Stansbury, Warren, 8/21/1880-1/6/1902
Stansbury, Wm. S., 3/4/1853-10/9/1920
Stansbury, Sue F., wife, 6/17/1852-11/1/1936
Kreider, Amos, 6/14/1830-9/16/1880,50y3m2d
Shenk, Eliz A., 8/28d/1832-9/7/1907, 75y10d

Cramer, Amos, 1st Lt. Co. B 99 Rgt. PVI, 1836-1924
Cramer, Rose, wife, 1848-1891
Cramer, Edwin R., son, Co. K 7th Inf., (Span.-Amer. War), 1885-1921
Cramer, Ray, son, 1887-
Prowell, Florella Duffy, 1884-1966
Duffy, Frank, 1853-1941
Duffy, Leah Ann, wife, 1863-1934
Duffy, Raymond, son, 1887-1888
McClune, Maris H., 1834-1906
McClune, Florella, wife, 1844-1922
McClune, Curlus, 1872-1924
Evans, Hercules, 1855-1942
Evans, Hattie, wife, 1863-1901
Evans, infant, 1893-1893
Evans, Clyde, son, 1900-1901
Duffy, James, 1820-1903
Duffy, Agnes, wife, 1827-1893
Duffy, John, son, 1847-1917
Galen, James B., 12/5/1853-6/29/1930
Galen, Margaret J., 5/30/1853-2/3/1929
Galen, Elvin G., son, 3/29/1880-10/6/1904
Alexander, Frances, d. 8/28d/1910, 75y
Alexander, John, husband, d. 1/30/1905, 75y
Hagen, Davis, 2/3/1847-11/29/1917
Hagen, Angeline Heeps, wife, 11/29/1840-1/21/1907
Robinson, F. T., erected by IOOF lodges, 1840-1915
Duffy, Charles H., 1870-1954
Duffy, Mary M., wife, 1876-1944
Duffy, Edwin L., son, 1899-1929
Winters, George, 1856-1926
Winters, Eliz., wife, 1860-1922
Winters, Edward M., 1895-1938
Winters, I. Clayre, Lt. Navy Nurse Corp WWII, 1905-
Stokes, Sarah R. Sellers, mother, 1885-1963
Stokes, Daniel, father, 1883-1956
Stokes, Harry D., s/o Dan & Rettie, 1911-1938
Hart, Harry O., 1884-1966
Hart, Della R. Dorsey, wife, 1885-1973

Row 6
Brenberger, Henry, Sr., 1/15/1812-7/1/1877, 65y5m16d
Brenberger, Catharine, wife, 8/9/1818-6/29/1865, 46y10m20d
Cramer, Elizabeth B., 1840-1911
H.E.
Heeps, Augustus, 1851-1938

Heeps, Margaret, wife, 1849-1940
Heeps, Daniel E., 1873-1949
Heeps, Ada R., 1876-1962
Heeps, infants, s. & d./ Aug. & Margt.
Heeps, M. Luella, d/o Wm. & Mary, d. 7/30/1885, 13y4m27d
Alexander, Rollandis A., 4/22/1862-1/17/1944
Alexander, Barbara, wife, 9/7/1863-4/14/1946
Heckey, Dora May, d/o Geo. W. & Eliz., 6/19/1863-12/3/1869, 6y10m24d
Heckey, George W., father, 1859-1948
Heckey, Eliz. H., mother, 1861-1938
Heckey, Dora M., 1883-1889
Heckey, Walter F., 1886-1900
Heckey, infant, 1895-1895
Heckey, George C., 1895-1969
Hieronymus, Rebecca Fares, 1887-1949
Fares, Charles A., May 1880-Aug 1899
Hagen, John, d. 4/15/1930, 89y8m4d
Hagen, Emma C., wife, d. 7/29/1901, 49y9m12d
Doulin, B. Frank, 1870-1944
Doulin, Ella J., wife, 1874-1945
Doulin, B. Frank, Jr., son, 1899-1900
Doulin, Harry W., son, 1912-1929
Keller, John W., 4/1/1840-5/3/1922
Keller, Elizabeth, wife, 5/30/1835-8/1/1906
Duffy, Albert, 1850-1923
Duffy, Viola E., 3/8/1865-11/2/1947
Duffy, James B., 10/3/1857-9/1/1910, 53y
Lindeman, Howard, 1883-1974
Lindeman, Harriet E. Hackman, wife, 1883-1913
Lindeman, Wm. Edgar, son, 1913-1913
Karr, John A. B., 1868-1965
Karr, Fannie C. Linderman, wife, 1863-1950
Karr, infant son, d. 4/13/1901, 1d
Winters, A. Lewis, father, 1886-1948
Winters, Ella M., mother, 1896-1973
Clements, H. Porter, 1898-1951
Clements, Myrtle, wife, 1900-1972

Row 7
___, Annie M., baby stone, no dates
___,___, baby stoned, can not read
McAfee, Thomas, 2/2/1857-12/26/1932
McAfee, Elizabeth, wife, 6/19/1855-9/5/1911
McAfee, Rebecca Mae, 1878-1961
Parker, Wm. 12/29-1821-3/5/1891, 69y2m6d

Parker, Rebecca, wife, 3/22/1822-2/2/1891, y m10d
Parker, Edward F., Mex.-Amer. War, d. 6/1892, 75y
Galen, James, brother, botanist, 3/23/1840-11/29/1906, 66y9m6d
Galen, Nancy Armstrong, mother, w/o Edward Galen, 8/20/1812-
   3/22/1896, 77y7m2d
Griffith, Albert, 1887-1898
Griffith, Chester, son, d. 10/1879, 12y10m15d
Lewis, Jacob, 1856-1935
Lewis, Annie, wife, 1857-1950
Lewis, Ethel, 1890-1935
Lewis, Stella, 1879-1899
Lewis, Marvin, 1883-1889
Lewis, Leroy, 1887-1889
Lewis, Ada L., 1881-1882
Lewis, Alfred, 1886-
Moss, J. Frank, 1862-1932
Moss, Frances E., wife, 1868-1937
Moss, Emma Evalene, dau., 5/23/1889-3/7/1891
Villee, Ada Moss, 1891-1973
Villee, Edgar R., 1883-1971
Eshleman, David G., 1881-1966
Eshleman, Wyoma K., wife, 1881-1971
Eshleman, Wm. M., son, 8/1/1902-11/15/1902
Good, Ephram, s/o Charles & Della, 9/29/1911-9/26/1914
Nordsick, Wm. A., 1917-1918
Nordsick, Edward F., 1927-1928
Nordsick, Anna E., 1885-1918
Shoff, Virginia H., w/o J. Chester, 1896-1918
Mundorff, Eliz. Herr, 1865-1942
Mundorff, George F., 1890-1945
Mundorff, Minnie E., 1892
Mundorff, George F. 1923
Mundorff, Franklin, 1916
Mundorff, Elizabeth, 1917
Mundorff, G. Franklin, father, 9/13/1854-4/16/1919
Tominson, Emanuel F., father, 1873-1929
Tominson, Maggie A., mother, 1864-1943
Tominson, Ross E., son, 1898-1951
Tominson, Ruth E., dau., 1903-
Murphy, Marjorie E., no stone, funeral marker, 1943-1969
Harman, Verna F., mother, 1913-
Harman, Harry E., father, 1910-1964

Row 8
Fares, John H., 11/9/1861 - _/9/1929

Fares, Elizabeth S., 10/20/1857-3/20/1922
Fares, Margie R., dau., 2/5/1875-4/17/1879
Kendig, Benjamin F., 5/3/1857-10/18/1940, 83y5m15d
Kendig, Miller J., wife, 2/22/1863-4/3/1900, 37y1m17d
Kendig, Thomas F., 5/1/1882-10/20/1897, 15y5m19d
Kendig, Mary E., 8/22/1888-10/11/1897, 9y1m19d
Shirk, Wm., 8/1/1857-2/25/1884/36y6m21d
Fulton, Raymond P., 2/19/1887-4/15/1947
Fulton, Anna S., 3/26/1891-12/16/1966
Hackman, Benjamin F., 1852-1933
Hackman, Susan A., 1864-1918
Hackman, John M., 1850-1929
Hackman, Elizabeth, 1827-1889
Hackman, Christian, 1826-1889
Hackman, Jacob, son, 1869-1870
Evans, George R., 1/25/1825-5/5/1913
Evans, Susan, wife, 9/13/1828-5/3/1907
Massey, Joseph P., 4/17/1856-4/20/1916, 60y3d
Massey, Annie M., wife, 5/26/1855-12/29/1909, 54y6m27d
Doran, Mary H., 1893-1975
Appleton, Maris L., father, 1889-1959
Appleton, Myrtle Witmer, mother, 1890-
Appleton, Mildred, dau., 1928-
Appleton, Helen W., dau., 1915-
Appleton, John C., 1885-1965
Appleton, Annie, wife, 1884-1947
Appleton, William M., 1860-1948
Appleton, Ellie E., wife, 1860-1931
Appleton, Blanche, dau., 1887-1963
Appleton, William E., son, 1904-1979
McCauley, Harry B., father, 1863-1924
McCauley, Margaret W., mother, 1865-1919
McCauley, Jasper W., Sgt. 23rd Field Hosp. US Army, WWI, 1894-1949
Miller, Charles D., 1904-
Miller, Thelma E., 1908-1970
Clements, H. Gerald, Sgt. 6th Ord. Med. Maint. Co., WWII, 1920-1957
Clements, Kathleen Stauffer, wife, 1921-
Clements, Hugh Gregory, son, 3/23/1950-11/1965

Row 9
Shirk, Amos, brother, 3/25/1838-10/14/1897
Smith, Florence, d/o George & Anna, 6/2/1890-10/28/1897
Heeps, Henry, Co. H 203 Regt. PV, 7/27/1847-2/11/1919
Heeps, Catharine A., wife, 8/121/1851-1/5/1902
Brenberger, George M., 1874-

Brenberger, Mary E. Heeps, wife, 1879-
Brenberger, Harry Martin, son, 1903-1904
Bruce, Earl Victor, 5/15/1882-8/29/1902
Bruce, Laura, mother, 1/13/1860-10/11/1907
Bruce, Amos F., father, 11/16/1856-2/4/1919
Trimble, Thomas J., father, Co. G 21st Pa. Cav., Co. D 122 Inf., 3/7/1837-
    1/12/1919
Trimble, Harriet M., mother, 11/24/1848-8/31/1915
Lefever, Charles A., 1870-1950
Lefever, Estella A. Trimble, wife, 1872-1945
Lefever, Thomas R., son, 1916-
Kurtz, George M., 4/23/1824-11/19/1909
Kurtz, Amelia, wife, 7/21/1833-6/16/1906
Kurtz, Emma M., dau., 1869-1918
Kurtz, Mary A., dau., 1866-1945
Kurtz, Charles A., 1872-1952
Kurtz, Christie, wife, 1873-1917
Kurtz, Arthur E., 1905-
Kurtz, Mary M. Wiggins, wife, 1905-1942
Kurtz, Allen Fredrick, son, 1931-
Funk, Ray E., 11/12/1884-
Funk, Myrtle, wife, 9/16/1882-9/15/1966
Funk, Martin A., son, 12/1/1909-1/3/1929
Funk, Ray A., Jr., son, 8/3/1911-11/1/1933
Funk, Theodore R., son, 3/19/1919-10/24/1940
Silverthorn, Ivan, 1858-1930
Silverthorn, Mary Todd, wife, 1862-1959
Silverthorn, Paul, great grandson, 1934-
Silverthorn, Ida E., 7/7/1888-6/26/1972
Silverthorn, Ivan E., 12/15/1890-4/21/1967
Silverthorn, Charles E., 11/11/1900-
Silverthorn, Mildred Holloway, wife, 7/14/1898-
M.M.S.
O.C.R., small stones (foot?)
Trimble, William R., 1865-1924
Trimble, Mary B., wife, 1872-1921

Row 10
Long, Julius, d. 9/30.1889, 54y
Oldham-Evans, Elizabeth, 1854-1935
Oldham-Evans, William A., 1862-1891
Oldham-Evans, Jacob, infant son, d. 1890
Evans, Elmer, 1855-1933
Fisher, Anna Myers, 1836-1893
Fisher, Fredrick B., Co. B 1st Md Lt. Art., d. 3/10/1915

Fisher, Annie M., wife, 5/26/1854-10/15/1918
Skethway, T. Chockley, 5/17/1879-12/19/1957
Skethway, Annie Naomi, 6/24/1886-8/17/1919
M.J.K., foot stone
Miller, Samuel W., 1856-1940
Miller, Mary Reese, wife, 1858-1937
Miller, Lloyd T., son, 1884-1907
Miller, L. Paul, 1898-1930
Miller, Caroline M., wife, 1903
Herr, Benj. F., 1/24/1860-5/19/1908
Herr, Laura L., wife, 3/26/1866-3/20/1936
Herr, Walter R., father, 1891-1966
Herr, M. Emma, mother, 1893-1916
Herr, Mabel M., 1892-
Trimble, William, 1863-1926
Trimble, Anna Gamber, wife, 1868-1962
Trimble, Olive M., 10/10/1886-8/4/1967
Trimble, Addison J., 3/8/1887-12/27/1966
Clark, Thaddeus J., Co. D 364 Eng. Div., 1896-1951
Clark, Anna S., wife, 1893-1934
Melott, Ira, 1895-1965
Melott, Cleo H., 1902-1959

Row 11
Campbell, Norman E., 1911-1976
Campbell, Mary E., wife, 1915-
Campbell, Michael P., son, 1947-1966
Walton, Earl, 1891-1978
Armstrong, Aldus E., 2/21/1880-8/21/1969
Rhoades, Samuel F., 1883-1948
Rhoades, Mabel E., 1900-1957
Graham, William B., 1849-1924
Brubaker, Clayton I., father, 1880-1956
Brubaker, Laura W., mother, 1881-1970
Brubaker, Theodore, 1908-1919
Shiffer, John E., father, WWI, 1891-1975
Shiffer, D. Pearl Lefever, mother, 1897-1973
Shiffer, Harriet E., dau., 1926
Barr, William W., father, 1858-1919
Barr, Mary Emma, mother, 1862-1926
Barr, W. Earl, son, 1891-1942
Barr, J. Calvin, son, 1883-1955
Herr, David Huber, 1889-1954
Herr, Lillie L. Barr, wife, 1891-
Null, Walter S., 1865-1923

Null, Martha A., 1864-1944
Null, Marvin S., 1898-1954
Null, Rellie E., wife, 1895-1976
Carter, John O., 8/19/1909-11/22/1970
Carter, Reba Funk, wife, 6/16/1913-
Diehl, Donald K., 1925-
Diehl, Dorcia Kilby, wife, 1930-
Diehl, Garren E., 10/29/1949 - 8/20/1965

Row 12
Herr, Harold E., 1913-1967
Herr, Verna M., 1914-
Evans, Ward Vinton, scientist & teacher, 1880-1957
Kohler, John, 1907-1956
Kohler, Kathryn, 1911-
Shaubach, James S., husband, WWII, 1914-1969
Shaubach, Kathryn Nordsick, wife, 1911-
Wissler, Charles D., father, 1918-
Wissler, Edna M. Null, mother, 1919-
Wissler, Robert A., son, 1941-1959
Wiggins, Clair T., 12/30/1919-4/27/1953
Wiggins, May A. Funk, wife
Sides, Clyde S., husband of Mary Funk Wiggins, 1910-1976
Harkcom, Willard F., father, 1912-
Harkcom, Violet M., mother, 1914-
Harkcom, Dale W., son, 1945-1964
Kunkle, Robert A., 1937-1954

Row 13
Warfel, Gregory Scott, s/o H. Gary & Shirley, 12/15/1962-12/22/1962
Henry, Ivan C., 1889-1960
Gainer, William V., 12/6/1900-4/3/1958
Gainer, Alice Herr, wife, 12/8/1902-
Gainer, Margaret E., dau., 6/18/1924-8/8/1967
Gainer, D. Lester, son, 12/6/1921-
Mueller, Michael J., 10/23/1891-6/28/1976
Mueller, Lestie A., wife, 3/30/1893-2/9/1956
Weitzel, Paul W., 8/23/1904-11/5/1966
Weitzel, Anna Eshleman, wife, 9/19/1906-

Row 14
Stokes, Charles, 1916-1978
Stokes, Elsie B., 1918-1978
Root, Terry L., 6/20/1958-12/28/1968
McKinley, Robert C., father, 1907-1967

McKinley, Daisy Minnick, mother, 1905-

RAWLINSVILLE MENNONITE CHURCH CEMETERY, 1946/1947 - 1978
Compiled by Jenne Renkin, April 1978

The church is 1 1/2 miles from Rawlinsville. A stone stands giving the date of the church as 1946-47. There are only five rows of graves with a few stones in each row. It is 1/8 mile from the 1742 Muddy Run Presbyterian Church and Cemetery. The old church has disappeared.

Row 1
Shotzberger, John, son, 8/18/1930-8/12/1949
Shotzberger, Paul K., Jr., 9/2/1927-
Shotzberger, Paul K., Sr., 3/28/1906-4/10/1974
Burkey, Eleanor M., 7/4/1933-8/15/1952
Nau, Florence, 1900-1957
Nau, Charles Henry, Sr., 1880-1950
Peltzer, George L., 1950-
Kilby, Louis J. Father. 1890-1960. Della T. Mother. 1892-1968

Row 2
Hess, Amos, 1914-1976
Hess, Alma Leahman, wife, 1914-1952
Hess, Esther Martin, wife, 1914-
Groff, Willis K., 1895-1973
Groff, Frances, wife, 1895-
Figueroa, Ana, 1961-1961
Figueroa, Rosa, 1960-1960
Greene, George E., QM T.C. WWII, 1906-1960
Pulfrick, William, 1887-1964

Row 3
Wood, Robert W., 7/22/1908-6/26/1968
Wood, Esther, 4/12/1916-
Reedy, Cleo W., no stone, funeral marker, 1914-1976
Reedy, Philip, Sr., 8/18/1882/26/1968
Reedy, Julia M., 4/29/1892-5/25/1961
Brecjbill(?), Carol Jane, d/o H. Melvin & Anna Ruth, 1965-1972

Row 4
Thomas, Sandy P., 6/15/1895-3/13/1959
Thomas, Ella E., 10/12/1900-3/18/1972
Farmer, Marion A., uncle, 6/4/1912-7/4/1969

Creasy, John P., no stone, funeral marker, 1900-1972
Osborne, Emma, mother, 8/11/1919-2/23/1958
Hess, Benjamin H., 1939-1972
Hess, Joyce Weaver, wife, 1941-
Stotzman, Joseph, no stone, funeral marker, 1915-1977

Row 5
Thomas, Sandy, 1896-1969
Creasy, Frank D., no stone, funeral marker, 1915-1975
Groff, Myron D., no stone, funeral marker, 1966-1977

CLEARFIELD M. E. CHURCH CEMETERY
Clearfield United Methodist Church, Rev. Ernest George, Pastor

This cemetery is located 11 miles from Lancaster, in Providence Twp. on Rawlinsville Road, 1 2/10 miles from Smithville, ca. 2 miles to Rawlinsville. It has 20 rows. Oldest stone readable - 1810, newest - 1973

The following inscriptions were read right to left from nearest to Church, going down the slope.
Recorded: October-November 1973 by Jenne Renkin

Row 1
Drumm, Samuel H., f., s/o Peter & Eliz., 1864-1925
___, Catharine Ellen, d/o Loddowick & Marg., 11/21/1815-4/30/1816, 5m9d
G.E.M.
Hess, John B., f., 9/18/1822-11/16/1878, 56y11m28d
Hess, Elila, m., w/o John B., 11/28/1827-9/5/1857, 29y9m8d
Hess, John W., s/o John B., d/10/29/1847, 8m11d
E.H.
J.B.H.
Wilson, Catharine E., sister, dau/John & Jane, 9/18/1840-4/12/1866, 22y6m24d
Wilson, John M., brother, s/o John & Jane, 9/30/1838-1/16/1859, 20y3m16d
Weidlich, Susanna, w/o Godfreid, d. 7/5/1866, 34y8m5d
Weidlich, inf. s/o J. W. W.
Weidlich, Godfreid, 2/17/1828-2/25/1901, 73y8
Miller, Albert E., 1877-1954
Miller, Henry C., 1847-1958
Miller, Henriette, his w., 1852-1917
Miller, William T., 1881-1958
Miller, Sarah E., 1872-1959
Peters, Sarah, 1834-1906 [on Miller stone]

Row 2

Reinhart, Almon F., 1858-1935
Reinhart, Ada E., 1862-1942
Reinhart, Michael R., 1891-1906
Reinhart, A. Cletus, 1896-1962
Reinhart, Ada E., 1903-1919
Miller, Aldus E., f., 10/10/1861-1/4/1914
Miller, Annie E., m., 9/6/1863-9/16/1916
Miller, Martha Irene, d/o Aldus, 1/9/1890-12/18/1895, 5y11m9d
Miller, Harry J., s/o Aldus, 8/27/1885-12/25/1885, 3m6d
Lyons, William B., 8/31/1839-1/19/1910
Lyons, Elizabeth, 12/15/1833-2/25/1910
Lyons, d/o William B., 3/15/1877-4/7/1883, 6y22d
Creamer, Elias, 1872-1955
Creamer, Annie Lyons, w., 1872-1951
Creamer, Ernest, 1894-1894
Creamer, Earl, 1894-1894
Creamer, Harry W., 1899-1904
Creamer, Reba M., 1902-1902
George, Vernon D., h., 1898-1959
George, Clare Creamer, 1895-1969
Creamer, David E., f., 1868-1898
Creamer, Mary R., m., 1871-1941
Light, Orrin Chester, d. 3/21/1969
Light, Edna M. Creamer, w., d.11/23/1966
S.J.D.
___ Sarah Jane, dau., unreadable, 1y
Drumm, Peter, f., 4/24/1814-10/13/1866
Drumm, Elizabeth A., m., 4/21/1824-4/28/1898
M.L.B.
Brown, Margaret A., our m., 10/1/1841-6/17/1882
Hill, William, s/o Wm. A. & Lizzie M., 1877-1937
Hill, Lizzie, m., dau/Peter & Eliz. Drumm, 1856-1919
Drumm, George O., bro., s/o Peter & Eliz., 1847-1923
M.O'N.
A.O'N.
O'Nail, Agnes w/o Hugh, d. 3/21/1853, 39y7m7d
O'Nail, Margaret, w/o Charles, d. 5/1/1859, 83y
O'Nail, Hugh, f., 7/21/1813-4/12/1876, 63y
McAfee, Margaret, 6/11/1779-7/9/1875
McAfee, Ann, 10/29/1804-12/11/1894, 90y1m13d
Langram__, Levi, 5/8/1811-10/_/18-, 15y7m15d
C.H.
Groff, Benjamin F., 1905-1909
Ford, Mary A. Groff, 1909-

Groff, Esther L., inf. d/Benj. & Mary, 4/13/1939
Groff, Frank, inf. s/o Benj. & Mary, 2/19/1934
Miller, Lewis G., 1863-1933
Miller, Emma F., w., stone flush with ground, 1870-1956

Row 3
Creamer, Emmet A., 1862-1944
Creamer, Annie R., 1865-1957
Creamer, Florence E., 1891-1904
Reinhart, Maris M. R., 1872-1942
Reinhart, Rebecca, his w., 1881-1913
Reinhart, Lydia A., his w., 1869-1934
Hart, Millar, 5/18/1853-2/9/1892, 38y8m21d
Hart, Viola May, d/o Millar & Sarah, 1888-1890, 1y8m29d
Kreider, Elias, f., 1851-1913
Kreider, Sophie, m., 1859-1882
Kreider, John & Mary, children, 1878-1882
Creamer, Walter A., 9/30/1865-11/9/1908
Creamer, Elizabeth L., his w., 12/13/1868-6/4/1958
Creamer, William L., s., 1894-1894
J.R.D.
Duke, John R., GAR, 4/25/1825-8/17/1865, 40y3m22d
Miller, Eve, w/o Jacob, 10/11/1826-1/8/1849, 23y4m27d
McAfee, David Howen, s/o David & Catha., 2/2/1860-1/9/1864, 2y11m7d
McAfee, Philena, d/o David & Catha., d. 9/30d/1851, 1y8m27d
McAfee, Catharine, w/o David, d. 2/15/1866, 37y9m20d
Keffer, William A., d. in Mil. Hosp., GAR, d. _/14/1864, 21y5m16d
Laird, Elizabeth, 11/1/1813-3/14/1897
Eyth, Theodosia, 2/22/1825-4/30/1874
Thompson, Tilghman, d. 1/_/1864, 60y
Newport, Elizabeth, w/o Samuel, for 60 yrs. a member of M.E. Church,
    11/11/1808-3/19/1886, 78y4m8d
Newport, Samuel, 8/4/1822-3/28/1903, 80y7m24d
H.L.T.
Thompson, Hiram L., Co. I, 122 Pa. Vol, GAR, d. 1/16/1902, 77y8m8d
Miller, Addie N., w/o John F. Miller, m., 9/14/1873-11/14/1915
Miller, John B., s/o John F. & Addie, 5/8/1913-8/21/1917
Groff, Benjamin M., f., 1876-1944
Groff, Martha Miller, m., 1889-1949
Fisher, Dora M., no stone, funeral marker, 1924-1973
Miller, Harry C., 1905-1973
Miller, Frances A., 1907-1936
LeFever, Victor M., f., 1906-1971
LeFever, Edith T., m., 1910-
LeFever, Edmund J., s., 1928-1939

LeFever, Arthur E., husband, seaman 2nd GL, WWII, 1927-1967
Creamer, Ray C., f., 1886-1970
Creamer, Blanche U., m., 1887-1958

Row 4
Heiney, Harry, 1854-1926
Heiney, Alice Jones, his w., 1859-1944
Heiney, Ida Maud, their dau., 1894-1895
Hill, Enos, f., 11/18/1880-5/26/1966
Hill, Goldie Heiney, m., 12/21/1879-6/22/1963
 father
 mother
1/2 row back in front of #9 row 5
Hart, Benjamin F., s/o Allen T. & Katie, 2/6/1881-8/2/1881, 5m26d
Hart, Allen J., our brother, 2/20/1857-10/20/1881, 24y8m
Hart, Leah, our m., w/o Simon, 3/9/1821-8/2/1888, 64y4m29d
Hart, Simon, our f., 11/27/1828-9/4/1905, 76y9m7d
Long, Joseph M., 1856-1944
Long, Naomi J. Conrad, his w., 1864-1940
Long, infant s., 1883-1883
(McFalls, Wm.)
Field stones
Hart, Benjamin, d. 4/20/1841, 15y4m4d
Hart, Mary, d/o Benj. & Eliz., d. 12/30/1852, 18y3m27d
Hart, Barbara, d/o Benj. & Eliz., d. 4/23/1859, 19y9m25d (E)
Elliott, Benjamin H., (boxwood covers it), 1865-
Elliott, Mifflin E., 1815-1883
Elliott, Isabella W., his w., 1824-1886
Elliott, Fleming, 1851-1851
Field stones
Elliott, Geo. W., 1852-1853
Elliott, Marian, 1852-1856
Elliott, Mary, 1856-1858
Elliott, Emmet, 1858-1859
Elliott, John, 1857-1861
Elliott, Anna Lettie, 1867-1871
Elliott, Benj. F., 1865-1971
F.E.
G.W.E.
Elliott, Fleming, s/o M. & I., d. 5/3/1851, 3m27d
Elliott, George, s/o M. & I, d. 1/3/1853, 2y17d
Lyne, Henry, d. 1/3/1853, 48y10m2d
Lynes, Elizabeth, 7/14/1802-12/14/1883, 81y5m
Miller, Peter, f., 2/22/1838-2/15/1913
Miller, Mary, m., 5/18/1836-5/9/1911

Miller, Charles L., 4le, 10/27/1884-12/8/1911
Miller, Anna Mae, dau., 3/9/1910-10/3/1920
LeFever, Landis, 11/7/1889-10/23/1918, 29y
Stauffer, H. Clayton, f., 9/27/1876-9/26/1917, 41y
Stauffer, Annie E., m., 12/7/1884-3/4/1920, 36y
Rhoads, Charles F., 9/3/1875-12/8/1962
Rosser, Andrew P., 1903-1953
Rosser, Myrtle, his w., 1905/1956
Rosser, Phyllis A. West, 1935-1937
Darlins, Mamie, d/o M. L. & Florence Reese, 3/15-18/1914, 3d
LeFever, Edmund E., 1885-1941
LeFever, Hettie M., 1886-1959
Miller, Walter H., hus., 1901-1962
Miller, ___, w/o Walter, 1901-1960
Gerlitzki, Charles E., Sr., f., 1903-1972
Gerlitzki, ___, m., 1903-

Row 5
Jones, Samuel, f., h/o Martha, 5/21/1830-6/21/1891, 61y1m
Jones, Martha, m., w/o Samuel, 7/24/1835-4/18/1901, 65y8m24d
Jones, Isaac, h., 11/8/1825-3/24/1897, 71y4m16d
Jones, Elizabeth, 5/12/1841-4/28/1929, (J)
McFalls, William E., s/o Aldus & Eliz., 1892-1/13/1893, 9m20d
McFalls, Aldus W., s/o Aldus & Eliz., 8/11/1900-12/7/1900, 3m23d
McFalls, William H., 11/23/1846-3/20/1899, 54y4m7d
McFalls, Susan, his w., 1/19/1849-9/11/1924, 75y7m22d
McFalls, Cora, d/o Wm. H. & Susan, 7/17/1883-12/23/1883
McFalls, William W., f., 11/10/1875-2/3/1920
McFalls, Rella, E., m., 5/9/1885-12/7/1961
McFalls, William A., s/o William & Rella, 4/8/1906-12/10/1906
McFalls, Eva C., d/o William & Rella, 5/22/1911-8/28/1911
McFalls, Walter W., s/o William & Rella, 8/28/1910-9/23/1910
Winters, C. Columbus, brother, 2/11/1858-12/15/1908, 49y, (Wm. Falls)
Wirth, Serenus, s/o Paul & Abbigail, 9/9/1981-, 8y1d
Wirth, Aaron, s/o Paul & Abbigail, 7/26/1874-, 8y, no date given
Wirth, Paul, f., 1841-1933
Wirth, Abigail, m., 2841-1934
Spence, John B., our f., b. in Ireland, 11/4/1790-4/6/1867, 76y3m2d
Spence, Barbara, 8/20/1796-9/1/1865, 69y10d
Spence, Gabriel, d. 1/11/18_6, 20y3m3d
Spence, Lodowick, d. 11/2/1815, 5y6m6d
Spence, Barbara, w/o Ulich, d. 4/1/18__, 64y10m18d
B.P.
M.H.
Hart, Henry, f., d. 10/25/1861, 61y5m12d

Hart, Elizabeth, w/o Henry, m., d. 7/14/1896, 76y8m2d
B.H.
Hart, Anna, d/o Henry & Elizabeth, 10/14/1847-4/7/1870, 22y5m23d
Hart, Mary, d/o Henry & Elizabeth, 10/14/1847-11/29/1929
Koble, Eliza., sister..., 10/19/1827-3/17/1884, 51y1m28d
Koble, Elias, 9/15/1796-10/24/1865, 69y1m9d
Koble, Theressa B., w/o Elias, Sr., 7/26/1807-6/18/1858, 50y11m22d
Koble, William, s/o Elias & Theressa, d. 1/23/1856, 5y2m5d
Koble, Jacob, s/o Elias & Theressa, d. 1/_/1845, 2y5m2d
Field stone
Gontner, Mary W., 1844-1929
Gontner, Catherine Ellen, my sis., d/o Wm. & Esther, 4/16/1848-
   7/17/1870, 22y3m1d
Gontner, John Albricht, s/o Wm. & Esther, 7/14/1846-4/14/1847, 9m23d
Cantner, Wm., s/o Daniel & Holly, 9/2/1811-2/28/1848, 35y4m16d
Gontner, Esther Winters, w/o Wm., d. 10/4/1851, 33y8m27d
Field stone
Eckman, Albert, f., 8/18/1833-3/17/1910, 70y5m29d
Eckman, Fannie E., m., 12/9/1839-3/6/1928, 69y2m27d
Garden, Lizzie E., 11/8/1876-9/7/1960
Tomlinson, Wm. R., f., 1900-1951
Tomlinson, Blanche, m., 1907-
unmarked old stone
Ritter, Paul R., 2/9/1886-4/4/1970
Ritter, Mary Ethel C., 8/8/l1903-8/17/1953
Dougherty, Bernard, 1920-1967
Dougherty, Lee T., 1930-

Row 6
McFalls, Chester F., s/o Aldus & Emma E., 8/15/1893-4/16/1894
McFalls, Aldus E., 1/22/1871-6/6/1946
Field stone
Brenneman, Barbara, w/o Benj. S., 12/2/1822-12/4/1880, 59y
Cox, Harold M., s/o Mary A Bush, 4/11/1892-10/3/1903, 11y5m22d
Field stone
Finefrock, Harry P., s/o Franklin G. & L., 11/30/1877-6/_/1878, 1y6m29d
Henry, Michael R., f., 9/16/1873(?)-8/11/1891, 57y10m25d
M.K.H.
R.S.
4 field stones
Bruce, John, s/o John & Mary, d., 1/20/1837, 4m10d
Smith, Ellanora, 4/30/1868-11/8/1901
Smith, Albert, f., 7/24/1818-12/31/1897, 79y5m7d
Smith, Susan, w/o Albert, m., 3/5/1827-2/12/1888, 60y11m7d
Smith, Mary, d/o Albert & Susan, 4/19/1851-12/2/1861, 3m10d

Smith, Mary, w/o George Sr., d. 5/20/1855, 65y3d
Smith, George, d. 2/20/1846, 29y11m4d
S.
Rineer, Martin E., f., 1868-1956
Rineer, Harrison H., s/o Martin & Harriet, 12/27/1908-1/20/1909, 1m29d
Rineer, Harriet E., m., 1874-1938
2 field stones
Hess, Warren I., 1915-
Hess, Verna N., 1917-
Hess, Jay Barry, son, 1942-1942
Henry, William A., 1892-1960
Henry, Minnie M. Rinier, his w., 1894-1970
Shultz, Lillie E., 1887-1960
Shultz, Harry B., 1886-1966

Row 7
Miller, Samuel, 1834-1923
Miller, Barbara, his w., 1834-1885
Miller, Mary Jane, his w., 1838-1919
Jenks, Frances M., 1867-1904
Miller, Susan, 1819-1899
Evans, Scott, 5/5/1854-4/19/1928
Evans, Mary, his w., 12/26/1857-3/5/1941
Evans, Harrie, d/o Scott & Mary, 10/19/1885-7/15/1891, 5y8m26d
Shroad, Mary, mem. of this ch. 60y, 6/20d/1794-9/19/1877, 83y5m
M.S.
Ritchie, Frances A., w/o James M., 8/3/1854-1/1/1902, 48y
Ritchie, Minnie N., d/o James M., 6/21/1875-11/1/1878
Ritchie, James W., s/o James M., 7/7/1883-4/7/1884
Ritchie, Edward E., s/o James M., 11/7/1891-3/1/1892
2 field stones
McFalls, Ruth B., d/o John & Sue, 12/14/1897-10/4/1898
1 field stone
Harvey, Sue E., d/o Martin & Ida, 5/10/1900-4/23/1910
Moore, Rose A., w/o Daniel M., 12/25/1845-8/17/1874, 28y7m23d
Lighthiser, Henry, s/o John & Mary, d. 11/31/1848, 5y4m27d
Clark, Ann, w/o Barthomew, 9/25/1767-2/12/1845, 77y
2 field stones
Rice, Mary, d/o John & Jane, d. 3/28/1838, 20y6m10d
Drumm, Mary, w/o George, d. 1/5/1859, 61y18d
Drumm, George, d. 8/5/1854, 63y11d
Drumm, Sampson, s/o Samuel & Lizabell, d. 5/2/1850, 2y5m20d
Drumm, Martha Jane, w/o Samuel, d. 3/13/1861, 24y11m21d
Drumm, Samuel, Co. H. 79th Rgt. Pa. Vol., GAR, 11/3/1830-5/28d/1909,
   78y6m25d

2 field stones
Eckman, Elizabeth, w/o Henry, d. 1/8/1867, 82y
Barley, Mary, w/o John, d/o Henry Eckman, d. 9/27/1848, 34y5m2d
Snavely, Martha, w/o Henry, m., 7/28/1816-3/24/1900, 83y7m27d
Snavely, Henry, d. 6/2/845, 26y7m11d
Snavely, Henry, s/o Henry, d.d 5/4/1845, 3m1d
Evans, Jacob, 1883-1949
Field stone
Evans, Sarah E., 1887-1937
Miller, Frank H., f., 1858-1930
Miller, Jennie, m., 1855-1942
Miller, Francis Irvin, 1880-1960
Sanders, Emma Miller, 1856-1931
Creamer, William, 1871-1939
Creamer, Mildred M. Heiney, his w., 1889-
Crouse, Harry L., 1865-1954
Crouse, Sarah E., his w., 1865-1946
Hoover, Elmer B., f., 1884-
Hoover, L. Romaine Kurtz, 1885-1958
Ressler, Leigh M., f., 10/10/1882-3/12/1961
Ressler, Minnie Fisher, m., 9/10/1884-4/14/1961
Clark, Ann Shoff, 1767-1845
McFalls, Sarah Clark, d/o Ann Clark, w. William McFalls, d. 1849, 60y

Row 8
Miller, Geo. A., 1858-1944
Miller, Martha, his w., 1853-1933
Smith, John, 1858-1924
Smith, Hettie A., his w., 1861-1937
Evans, Walter G., f., 1867-1931
Evans, Maggie B., m., 1873-1959
Rame, Mary Evans, dau., 1900-1949
Locke, Susan, d/o Wm. & Mary, d. _/_/1863, 17y3m11d
Locke, Mary, d/o Wm. & Mary
___, Debbie, d. 12/27/1862, 3m24d
Locke, Jane, w/o Thomas, 3/25/1778-1/23/1856, 76y9m29d
Locke, William, d. 4/_/1863, 63y4m9d
2 field stones
Creamer, Catharine, 3/15/1815-12/2/1903, 88y8m17d
C.C.
Creamer, Hannah, w/o Christian, 11/9/1795-2/11/1819, 35y3d
Creamer, Christian, rest of stone buried
G.C.
H.C.
Creamer, Hiram L., Corp., s/o - & -, GAR, 4/_/1841-7/20/1863, 22y6m11d

H. McF.
McFalls, Sarah, w/o William, d. Jan. 1849, 60y8m, rest of stone buried
McFalls, Margaret, w/o Henry, m., 1772-5/21/18<u>22</u>
Jones, Albert Elmer, 18__ - 18__
McFalls, Mary, d/o Henry & Rachel, <u>1</u>/3/1841-5/1/1842, 1y3m29d
McFalls, Oren, s/o Henry & Rachel, 7/21/1842-3/13/1843, 6m23d
McFalls, Rachel, w/o Henry, m., _/20/1805-2/10/1890, 86y5m21d
McFalls, Henry, f., 9/7/1803-7/18/1871, 68y10m11d
Brenneman, Christian, f., 6/12/1791-8/16/1871, 80y2m24d
(CB)
(CB)
Brenneman, Catharine, w/o Christian, m., 6/22/1806-1/15/1888, 81y6m23d
Brenneman, John, s/o Christian, 1/30/1813-5/20/1813, 3m21d
Brenneman, Catharine, d/o Christian, 6/18/1812-3/12/130, 17y
(CB)
(CB)
Armstrong, T. Jefferson, 1855-1933
Armstrong, Elizabeth, his w., 1856-1938
Armstrong, Daisey, 1877-1878
Armstrong, Grace, 1886-1887
Field stone
Nult, Leonard, 201st Pa. Inf. USA, 1900
(E.R.) broken
Field stone
Shenk, Harry C., (S), 1881-1910
Shenk, Emma N. Rineer, his w., 1892-
Shenk, Lottie, inf. dau., 1909
Shenk, Carrie, 12/1/1910-
Shenk, John, 8/10/1913-
Rineer, Fred K., 1902-1963
Rineer, Hattie M., 1912-
McFalls, John W., 6/27/1928-7/1/1928
McFalls, Della M., no stone, funeral marker, 1888-1971
Sigman, Emma E., m., 1899-1937
Sigman, William James, Jr., US Marine Corp., WWII, 1/19-1921-4/11/1948
Coble, David R., 1901-1964
Coble, Elsie M., 1903-
Smith, Harry M., 1884-1958
Smith, Anna L., his w., 1886-

Row 9
Heisler, Socratese M., h., 1867-1953
Heisler, Suie V. Conrad, m., 1869-1965
Brechbill, Clare Heisler, 1889-1952
Brechbill, Laban T., 1892-19__

Gaul, Martha E., 2/3/1906-
Shank, Hiram, 1/26/1828-10/10/1890, 62y8m11d
Shank, Mary, w., 4/20/1828-3/26/1888, 59y11m6d
Eisenberger, Elam, f., 9/16/1856-3/13/1923
Eisenberger, Susan, m., 3/9/1858-1/23/1943
Eisenberger, Charles M., inf., 4/17-8/17/1882, 4m
C.N.E.
Field stone
Conrad, John, f., 10/9/1833-4/4/1906, 73y
Conrad, Mary Breneman, m., w/John, 10/6/1837-1/16/1910, 73y
4 field stones
____ Elias, s/o Henry & ___, 2/11/1850-3/10/1851, 1y2m20d
Cully, James, d. 5/22/1865, 56y9m20d
3 field stones
Hart, Samuel, f., broken stone, 6/1/1811-8/21/1876, 67y2m20d
Hart, Susanna, w/o Samuel, m., 7/12/1813-5/20/1895, 81y10m8d
Hart, Barbara, d/o Samuel, 11/27/1844-3/22/1861, 16y3m25d
Hart, Catharine, d/o Samuel, 10/16/1849-7/25/1850, 9m9d
Newport, James, d. 8/11/1838, 55y6m5d
Newport, Esther, broken, d. 5/25/1879, 93y7m26d
Newport, Eliza, d. 4/3/182-, 10y5m18d
___, Elizabeth, w/o John, 2/28/1802-10/25/1850, 48y7m2d
Small stones buried in ground
A.W.
S.W.
A.W.
Warfel, Sarah, w/o Wm., 10/18/1829-3/3/1849, 19y1m12d
Wilson, John, f., broken, 6/25/1805-1/25/1881, 75y7m
Wilson, Jane, w/o John, m., 10/20/1800-11/26/1878, 78y1m6d
Spence, Gabriel, s/o John & Martha, d. 10/31/1846, 9m16d
Spence, Mary, d/o John & Martha, 4/6/1850-8/8/1850, 5m2d
Wilson, Catharine, w/o Benj., 4/1/1811-3/9/1853
Wilson, Benj., stone buried
Wilson, Barbara, d/o Benj., 2/12/18-0-4/22/18-0
Wilson, Jane, d/o Benj., d. 8/29/1840, 1y4m22d
Wilson, James, s/o Benj., d. 9/9/1842, 1y10m9d
Wilson, Jane, w/o James, our m., d. __/17/1872, 91y1m1d
Wilson, James, our f., d. 12/19/1851, 77y9d
Flawd, David, f., Co. D 59 Rgt. Pvt, GAR, 7/17/1845-2/2/1908, 65y5m15d
2 field stones
Flawd, Eliz, w/o David, 3/27/1843-9/19/1923, 80y5m22d
(F)
Field stone
Unmarked stone
Miller, Claude M., 1891-1974

Miller, Cora C., his w., 1895-1929
(M)
Priest, William M., f., 1896-1955
Priest, Anna M., m., 1898-1932
Priest, Emma G., w., 1914-1952
Jay Rohrer [owner of lot]
Priest, Marconus K., f., 1891-1951
Priest, Emma E., m., 1873-1957
Priest, Ira H., Cpl. WWI, flag, 1898-1971
Sensenig, John K., Holy Bible, 1868-1954
Sensenig, Annie L., 1870-1962
Trissler, Benj. F., 1895-1971
Trissler, Orello V., 1897-
Roach, Mary T., 1888-1958

Row 10
Armstrong, John K., f., 1/5/1857-8/8/1932, 75y8m3d
Armstrong, Mary E., m., 1/17/1858-6/22/1907, 49y5m5d
Armstrong, M. Wifield, s., 3/6/1881-1/19/1922
Armstrong, John K., ch/o J. & M. A., 7/16/1889-4/7/1890
Armstrong, Lottie, ch/o J. & M. A., 10/__/1886-7/2/1888
Armstrong, Chester A., 8/9/1891-1/9/1898, 6y5m
2 field stones
Locke, Abraham, f., GAR, 10/20/1837-11/10/1910
Locke, Nancy J., w/o Abraham, 6/8/1859-12/25/1900, 61y6m7d
Locke, Flora M., d/o Abraham, 7/19-8/20/1877, 1m1d
Wilson, Elizabeth H., m., w/o Josiah, 3/12/1807-2/25/1888, 85y11m3d
Clarkson, Rachel, 3/7/1808-4/11/1873, 65y1m4d
Noll, John, d. 7/29/1883, 5y6m4d
Coble, N___, s/o Martin & ___, d. __/__/1870, -y-m17d
Coble, Benjamin, s/o Martin & M__, 3/2/1849-9/6/1862, 14y4m17d
Coble, Samuel, s/o Martin & M__
Coble, Martin, s/o Martin & M__, __/24/1856-8/22/1859, 3y7m2d
Coble, Ann Eliz., d/o Martin & Maria, stone buried, d./ 10/20/1853, 2y-_m-
    d
Coble, Eliz., d/o John & Susan, __/17/l1853-8/5/1854
Coble, John, s/o John & Susan, __/10/1854-12/20/1854
Coble, Christian, s/o John & Susan, 5/27/1849-3/7/l1866, 16y10m13d
Coble, Susan, w/o John, 1/1/1828-11/28/1908, 80y10m21d
Coble, John, 5/11/1824-10/18/1899, 75y5m7d
Hart, John, f., d. 12/11/1899, 67y8m10d
Hart, Mary Ann, m., d. 12/17/1932, 92y5m22d
Hart, Sarah Martha, 1862-1949
Jackson, Annie Hart, 1868-1957
Hart, Maris L. H., 1860-1861

Hart, John C. H., 1870-1871
Mar__us, ___, s/o Geo. & ___, 3/12/1838-4/26/1848
Hart, William H., s/o Geo., d. 2/25/1850, 3__y7m30d
Hart, John, 5/31/1778-1/25/1853, 6__y7m25d
Hart, Barbara, w/o John, 4/8/1779___1/1852, 74y7m8d
Appleton, John, 4/25/1817-5/11/1878, 71y10d
Shirk, Mineva, d/o Amos & Martha A., d. 4/17/1881, 16y
Shirk, Samuel, s/o Amos & Martha A., stone buried
Milimer, Benjamin, s/o Benj. & Mary, d. 2/2/1843
5 field stones
Douglas, Ann, w/o Geo., d. 8/5/1876
A.D.
G.D.
2 field stones
Douglass, Geo., d. 4/8/1884, 75y
Douglass, Samuel, Co. K 181 D Cav. 1920
(W)
Warfel, Earnest R., s/o Henry H. & Anna, 9/26-10/2/1907
Warfel, Myrtle, d/o Henry H. & Anna, 4/8-12/23/1906
Miles, Jacob J., f., 1859-1929
Miles, Sarah E., 1860-1953
Miles, Ralph C., 1890-1948
Rohrer, Jay M., 1898-1971
Rohrer, Flora E., 1898-1961
Eshleman, Frank, 1889-1965
Eshleman, Ada Brubaker, 1890-1963
Eshleman, Annie M., 1896-1970

Row 11
Wiggins, Clayton, f., Pvt. Co. K 195th R., PV, 5/31/1846-6/3/1904, 59y
Wiggins, Harriet L., m., 7/5/1847-8/5/1921, 74y
Wiggins, Leroy S., 10/23/1898-7/28/1947
Wiggins, Wm. C., 1875-1963
Wiggins, Mazie M. Evena, 1878-1930
Kobel, Maria, m., 1/_5/1824-7/26/1910, 86y6m2d
Kobel, Martin, f., Co. I 195th Rgt. Pa. Vol., 8/21/1825-7/11/1891
Field stones
Krug, Ann, w/o Peter, broken, 7/16/1834-4/24/1886, 51y9m18d
Krug, Peter, 8/23/1822-1/19/1865, 45y4m26d
Krug, William, s/o Peter, 10/21/1858-5/18/1863, 5y7m7d
Krug, Lucy, d/o Peter, __/17/1860- __/12/1861, 1y25d
Krug, Martha Ann, d/o Peter, d. 11/20/1857, 4d
A.K.
2 field stones
Lee, Catharine, w/o Joshue, d. 3/21/1868, 81y9m30d

Urban, Benjamin F., Co. __, 79th Regt. P.I.V., in Goldsboro, NC, d. of
    wound received [on] 3/25/1865, d. 3/25/1865, 24y10m23d
Marks, Francina, d. 8.7.1857, 43y9m10d
Kirkwood, Thomas G., GAR, 6/21/1821-9/11/1882, 58y2m2d
Kirkwood, Henry O., s/o Thomas, d. 8/11/1861, 2m1d
Kirkwood, Susan, w/o Thomas G., stone buried, d. 7/23/1864, 30y10m8d
Kirkwood, Emma J., d/o Thomas G., d. __/__/1862, 3m
Kirkwood, Corinea J., d/o Thomas G., d. 7/10/1869, 2m20d
Kirkwood, R. Fulton, s/o Thomas G., d. 1/13/1857, 5m13d
Kirkwood, Jane, w/o Thomas, d. 12/26/1856, 66y1d
9 field stones
-.H.
Gonley, Emma Jane, d/o Wm. & Susan, 4/15/1847-7/11/1842, 2y2m28d
Gonley, Susan, w/o Wm., 10/25/1806-1/19/1872, 65y2m25d
Gonley, William, 8/4/1802-6/29/1864, 61y10m25d
Hart, Amos, 8/25/1826-10/15/1861, 25y10m25d
Smith, Henry, f., 1/14/1824-12/25/1907, 83y9m11d
Smith, Sarah A., w/o Henry, m., 2/5/1820-4/26/1882, 62y2m22d
Nagle, Emma M., m., w/o George, 4/23/1847-11/19/1866, 19y9m6d
Smith, John S., s/o Henry & Sarah, 8/16-10/18/1860
Smith, Charles, s/o Henry & Sarah, 8/6-10/18/1860
Smith, Arnold, f., d. 1/26/1871, 78y1m21d
Smith, Jemima, w/o Henry, 10/24/1830-1/29/1907, 76y3m5d
__, Sarah Ann, w/o __, 3/27/1827-2/21/1856, 20y6m25d
Jones, Benjamin F., 1854-1943
Jones, Mary J., his w., 1855-1930
J.W.
Jones, Charles E., 1/1/1884-11/17/1907, 23y16d
Sangrey, Ira D., f., 4/2/1884-6/20/1913, 29y2m18d
Field stone
Finefrock, Tobias, Rev., GAR, 2/24/1845-5/23/1916, 72y2m29d
Finefrock, Elmira, w/o Tobias, 5/21/1844-7/9/1912, 68y1m18d
Kreider, George M., 1878-1936
Kreider, Matilda A. Hessenauer, his w., 1892-1967
Carrigan, Benjamin, f., 1876-1956
Carrigan, Lottie M., m., 1874-1954
Doulin, Charles E., f., 1904-1973
Doulin, Dorothy M., m., 1907-1960
Henry, Ross B., 12/4/1894-11/17/1965, married 4/4/1916
Henry, Catharine C., 3/28/1899-

Row 12
Newcomer, Samuel, h., 2/6/1876-2/17/1914
Newcomer, Emma F., w., 12/15/1876-8/19/1962
Coble, Frank, f., 8/31/1856-12/4/1938

Coble, Henrietta, m., 11/6/1859-11/21/1938
Johnson, Howard S., 11/13/1882-10/7/1949
S.M.L.
2 field stones
Myers, Amos C., 1899-1931
6 field stones
Eshleman, Theophilus, 4/6/1859-6/23/1943
Eshleman, Emma Lyons, 7/18/1854-9/3/1918
C.M.F.
Smith, Henry, f., 6/27/1827-2/3/1907, 79y9m6d
Smith, Barbara, w/o Henry, m., 11/5/1825-1/26/1915, 89y2m21d
Smith, Simon Peter, s/o Henry & Barbara, 7/18-10/12/1858
Smith, John G., s/o Henry & Barbara, d. 12/24/1857, 4m23d
Drumm, Catharine E., 4/6/1855-10/27/1868
Drumm, Mary A., 12/4/1847-1/3/1867
Drumm, Amanda A. J.
Drumm, George W., f., GAR, 9/1/1824-7/31/1900
Drumm, Catharine, m., 6/16/1825-1/3/1901
Holshouse, Peter, Q.M. Sgt. Co. I 20 Pa. Cav., WWI.
Daily, Mary, grandmother, 1770-1857, 87y
Daily, Lydia, m., 4/15/1809-12/17/1893, 83y7d
Daily, Eliza, sister, d. 8/19/1876, 70y
4 field stones
E.D.
Eisenberger, Maris S., f., 1883-1961
Eisenberger, Katherine M., m., 1885-
Eisenberger, Charles L., s/o Maris, 6/8-7/1/1906
Eckman, Walter, 8/9/1914-3/17/1870
Eckman, Clara P., his w., 12/5/1878-7/20/1930
Myers, Benjamin, f., 1879-1921
Myers, Essie, 1888-
Heisler, Hiram, GAR, 4/2/1846-2/27/1933
Heisler, Annie, his w., 3/22/1844-6/20/1930
Myers, Benj. F., 1869-1941
Myers, Alice E., his w., 1858-1935
Myers, Harry F., s., 1886-1934
Myers, Jacob, WWI 304th Engr., 1890-1957
Kilburn, Charles M., 1907-1941
Kilburn, Ruth M., 1908-1963
Charles, Walter W., h., 1896-
Charles, Maude E., w., 1895-1968
Kauffman, Paul M., 2/2/1901-
Kauffman, Harriet E., 11/19/1901-

Row 13
Conrad, Charles W., 1872-1922
Conrad, Mazie K. Reinhart, his w., 1881-1921
Conrad, Claud R., s/o Charles & Mazie, d. 12/3/1908, 1d
Conrad, George W., s/o Charles & Mazie d. 2/18/1901, 1d
Conrad, Lawrence, 2/18/1901, 1d
Johnson, Cyrus, 1858-1931
Johnson, Laura, his w., 1860-1927
Johnson, Ella M., 3/23/1887-1/16/1901
Johnson, Park P., 6/2/1890-1/8/1901
Johnson, Naomi E., 12/20/1884-1/19/1901
Eshleman, John, f., 2/10/1827-5/7/1898, 71y2m27d
Eshleman, Mary Ann, w/o John, m., 10/__/1819-10/26/1882,
  69y
Eshleman, Jacob, 1/11/1802-8/13/1876, 72y2m14d
Eshleman, Esther, w/o Jacob, 8/18/1799-3/7/1876, 76y3m19d
Eshleman, Amos, s/o Jacob & Esther, 1/2/1826-12/11/1828, 2y10m29d
Eshleman, Hetty, m., 1837-1928
Eshleman, Amos E., s., 1867-1882
A.C.
Creamer, Aaron, 4/__/1813-2/14/1878, 65y10m
Creamer, Peter, f., 9/17-1828-2/3/1872, 43y4m16d
Creamer, Martha, w/o Peter, m., 1/10/1831-5/20/1910, 79y4m10d
Creamer, Mary Elizabeth, dau., 12/27/1867-1/20/1898, 30y23d
Creamer, Hiram A., s., 3/25/1859-2/10/1862, 2y10m15d
Creamer, Lillian F., dau., 9/1/1864-3/1/1866, 1y6m
Creamer, Barbara Alice, dau., 9/4/1861-3/24/1879, 17y3m20d
Creamer, Abraham, f., 3/17/1829-3/8/1916
Creamer, Fannie M., w/o Abraham, m., 3/10/1829-10/6/1895
Creamer, Alice C., 4/13/1856-9/24/1862
Creamer, C. Thompson, 3/17/1858-9/19/1862
Creamer, S. M___, 12/12/1860-9/14/1862
McFalls, Esther, 8/15/1810-7/12/1890, 79y10m28d
McFalls, Patrick, 1/28/1796-6/30/1865, 69y5m2d
McFalls, Jacob, 6/25/1838-10/24/1862, 25y3m9d
McFalls, John, 9/10/1845-8/20/1866, 20y11m10d
McFalls, Henry, 9/22/1840-1/19/1869, 28y3m21d
Drumm, Lorenso, s/o Isaac & Eliz., bro., 3/16/1849-4/15/1864, 14y10m29d
Drumm, Isaac, f., Co. B 78 Rgt. Ohio Vol., GAR, 11/18/1821-12/14/1873,
  52y16d
Drumm, Martha A., 3/5/1827-7/31/1910
Conradt, Charles, f., 1855-1922
Smith, Linda, 1857-1925
Musselman, John F., f., 9/19/1851-3/21/1923
Musselman, Laura A., m., 2/7/1849-11/30/1927

(F)
(E)
Evans, Abraham E., 1903-
Evans, Viola, Ros___, his w., 1906-
Evans, Jean Rosene, 1927-1927
Evans, Walter Grendecker, 1932-1936
Evans, Paul LeMayne, 1933-
Coble, Elmer, 1862-1937
Coble, Viola A. Winters, his w., 1867-1945
Eckman, Aldus J., f., 1849-1934
Eckman, Emma, m., 1858-1942
Eckman, Joseph W., 4/9/1887-8-19/1950
Eckman, Ella J., his w., 2/18/1882-11/26/1965
Eckman, Charles J., s., 8/9/1909-4/14/1940
Carrigan, Samuel E., 1904-
Carrigan, Susan M.
McFalls, 1907-1965
Henry, J. Russell, 1920-1969
Henry, Nina R., 1925- , this stone 1/2 between rows 12 & 13

Row 14
Kreider, Daniel K., 1849-1931
Kreider, Martha Jane Drumm, his w., 1852-1906
Kreider, Samuel H., ch., 1876-1905
Kreider, John M., ch., 1887-1911
Kreider, Daniel P., M.D., ch. interred Mt. Holly Spring, Pa.
3 markers
Petru, Wm. C., 1901-1971
Petru, Claire K., 1908-1971
Petru, Wayne C., 1947-1964
Snyder, Della C., 5/21/1885-5/11/1966
Rineer, Emma, w/o John, 3/3/1852-1/27/1903
Paes, Harry, f., 1863-1948
Paes, Ada F., m., 1861-1907
Paes, Claude H., s/o Harry & Ada, 3/25/1901-9/2/1903
Paes, Edna, infant d/o Harry & Ada, 3/5-9/1898, 4d
Sweigart, Felix, f., 8/26/1822-8/25/1898, 76y
Sweigart, Sarah A., w/o Felix, m., 11/21/1825-2/22/1904
Sweigart, George F., s/o Felix & Sarah, 6/26/1860-12/17/1863, 3y5m21d
Sweigart, Elmer E., s/o Felix & Sarah, 11/10/1864-1/12/1879, 14y2m2d
Kreider, Flora Bell, d/o Franklin & Mary D., 12/15/1876-1/12/1877, 28d
Journey, Susanna, w/o Wm. R. Journey, d/o Christian & Eliz. Kreider,
    3/2/1854-3/5/1875, 20y11m3d
Kreider, Christian, 1/15/1822-9/12/1865, 41y7m29d
Kreider, Elizabeth, 1/2/1822-11/10/1900, 78y10m8d

Eisenberger, Jacob, f., broken stone, 11/17/1826-2/23/1907, 80y3m6d
Eisenberger, Catharine, w/o Jacob, m., 8/18/1834-3/27/1874, 49y7m19d
Eisenberger, George W., s/o Jacob & Catharine, d. 2/27/1872, 5y3m2d
Eisenberger, Harry Clinton, s/o Jacob & Catharine, 8/20/1878-1/30/1879, 5m10d
Eisenberger, Samuel F., s/o Jacob & Catharine, 1861-1936
Drumm, Wm. Urie, s/o Peter & Eliz., f., Vol. to Co. D 2 Regt. Pa. Inf., re-en. Co. G 21 Regt. Pa. Cav., 1844-1932
Drumm, Laura J., m., 4/29/1847-7/29/1871
G.W.D.
C.D.
Drumm, J. Elmer, our son, 5/3/1858-5/28/1890
G. V. C.
___, Daisy Viola, d/o ___ & ___, 6/12-27/1884, 15d
Eberle, Amos H., 1884-1938
Eberle, Dora Rineer, his w., 1881-1950
Evans, Elmer, f., 1884-1939
Wissler, Daniel Herr, f., 5/7/1880-5/14/1947
Wissler, Sylvia Heiney, m., 4/13/1882-12/31/1945
Cramer, Milton R., f., Sp. Amer. War, flag, 1876-1947
Cramer, Mary A., m., 1877-1968
Quigley, William C., 1907-
Quigley, Margaret S., his w., 1902-1968
Long, Jeffrey Lynn, ch/o Charles V. & Evelyn M., d. 12/28/1963, 1d
Long, Susan Yvonne, ch./o Charles V. & Evelyn M., d. 12/28/1963, 2d

Row 15
Paes, Harry H., 1887-1937
Paes, Margaret E., his w., 1888-1961
Paes, inf. s/o Harry & Margaret, d. 5/14/1908
Paes, Wm. F., f., 1885-1960
Paes, Myrtle Miller, w/o Wm. F., 1885-1920
Paes, Helen Merie, d/o Wm. F. & Myrtle, 1907
2 field stones
McFalls, John C., s/o Wm. & H., 1/17/1871-6/22/1905, 34y5m5d
McFalls, Harriet, w/o William, m., 10/31/1828-9/26/1880
McFalls, William, 4/17/1831-8/11/1906, 74y4m14d
Brenneman, Mary Emma, d/o ___lman & Su__, d. 12/19/1867, 11y29d
Ruher, Frankie, s/o Amos & Martha, 12/19/1876-1/16/1878, 1y28d
Kepperley, John, Co. D 9th Pa. Cav., gov't. stone, 1885
Thomas, Albert, Co. I 64th Regt. Ohio Vol. Inf., 1834-1921
Thomas, Sarah J., 1833-1898
Gochnauer, infant d/o Jacob & Harriet
Gochnauer, Harriet, w/o Jacob, m., 6/21/1844-2/7/1869, 24y7m16d
Gochnauer, Jacob, h., GAR, 7/9/1842-10/18/1883, 47y4m9d

J.M.//E.M.//F.M.//M.M.
3 field stones
Klump, William W., 10/24/1859-2/27/1834[?]
A.D.
Shingler, Howard F. (Duke), 1903-1967
(Caroline)
Musselman, Harry C., 10/11/1887-1/3/1963
Musselman, Effie S., 4/18/1888-6/1/1948
(L)
(Groff)
Armstrong, Benj. F., f., WWI, 1898-1958
Armstrong, Elsie E., m., 1900-1964
Armstrong, John Rbt., s/o Benj F. & Elsie E., 11/11/1926-5/21/1949
Miles, Edward, 1885-1959
(Mylin)
Mylin, S. Miller, 1876-1968
Mylin, G. Gertrude, his w., 1884-1954

Row 16
Kreider, David, f., 1833-1904
Kreider, Martha M., m., 1841-1922
Kreider, J. Calvin, 12/22/1861-5/7/1934
Kreider, Milton S., 3/3/1879-10/6/1955
Barton, John H., h., Co. E 79th Rgt. Pa. Vol., 8/12/1841-3/29/1889,
    47y7m17d
J.H.D.
Field stone
Mowrer, Maggie, d/o Tobias & Eliz., 7/15-8/5/1887, 19d
Mowrer, Isaac, s/o Tobias & Eliz., 2/10-7/24/188, 5m14d
Mowrer, Emma Dora, dau/Tobias & Eliz., 5/12/1868___/__/1871, 3y17d
Bair, Emma, d/o John & Susan, 11/26/1867-2/22/1867, 1/3m12d
Bair, Susan, w/o John, 1/10/1846-2/26/1870, 24y1m16d
Miller, Frederick C., 3/19/1869-10/5/1930
Miller, Jacob C., 10/19/1862-4/23/1925
Miller, Samuel C., 11/14/1865-11/27/1923
Miller, Jacob, 5/22/1820-8/15/1892, 72y8m23d
Miller, Mary, w/o Jacob, 1/10/1828-2/17/1897, 69y4m7d
Vollrath, John A., f., 6/10/1809-8/25/1871, 62y2m15d
Vollrath, Maria S., 9/28/1811-3/23/1888, 76y6m13d
Miller, S., Co. I 7th Pa. Cav., gov't. stone, 1895
Miller, Eliza, w/o Socrates, 2/15/1818-11/21/1907, 89y9m16d
Micken, Chas., Co. H 2nd Pa. Cav., gov't. stone, 1906
Micken, Charles, f., 1846-1906
Micken, Mary M., m., 1850-1898
Micken, Eliz., d/o Charles & Mary, 1873-1892

Jones, Hiram, Co. G 79th Pa. Inf.
Jones, Ellenor, d. 3/3/1866, 19y10m3d
Micken, Aldus, 1878-1958
Micken, Margaret Donley, his w., 1898-1932
Weaver, R. Morris, 1903-
Weaver, Grace N., 1904-
Newcomer, Ruth H., 2/29/1912-
Loump, Abram B., f., 1895-1969
Loump, Mary M., m., 1896-1962
Loump, Dale E., s., 896 Anti Aircraft WWII, 1/25/1924-10/7/1950
Fritz, Norman A., s/o Wm. & E. Helanie, 8/9/1956-5/4/1959
Warfel, Carrie I., m., 1900-1960

Row 17
Newcomer, Isaac B., f., 9/15/1841-8/23/1915
Newcomer, Elizabeth, m., 4/5/1850-3/13/1924
Newcomer, Martha, d/o Is. & Lizzie, 12/17/1887-9/27/1898, 10y9m10d
Newcomer, William H., s/o Is. & Lizzie, 12/11/1872-2/3/1907, 34y2m22d
2 field stones
Reese, Albert, Co. H 79th Pa. Inf., GAR, gov't. stone, 1901
J.C.S.//M.E.//A.L.//M.S.//Field stone//A.S.//Field stone
McFalls, Margaret, 2/28/1795-2/24/1884, 88y11m24d
Moss, Susan, 8/4/1801-11/12/1885, 84y2m8d
Field stone
McCombs, Amos, Co. C 20th Pa. Cav., gov't. stone, GAR flag
Field stone
McCombs, Thom., Co. K 20th Pa. Cav.
Eckman, Clarence E., 2/24/1901-
Eckman, Esther, M., his w., 3/11/1905-11/15/1953
Micken, W. Martin, 4/4/881-
Micken, Clara B. Mylin, w., 12/13/1884-9/22/1969
(A)
Mylin, Holmes R., 1932-
Mylin, JoAnn M., 1938-1969

Row 18
O'Brian, Hannah R., m., 6/10/1872-10/28d/1909
Field stone
Gross, Wm. C., f., 11/11/1889-2/23/1972
Gross, Ellen M., m., 3/27/1899-10/31/1967
Dillich, Mary Ann, m., 5/7/1855-1/31/1883
Finefrock, Albert F., ch/o John & Mary, 1/4-12/31-1878
Finefrock, Effie K., ch/o John & Mary, 2/26-10/28/1877
Finefrock, Peter, f., 3/15/1800-10/18/1896, 96y7m18d
Finefrock, Susan, w/o Peter, m., 8/14/1813-9/13/1871, 78y4m19d

Brenbarger, Edward, s/o John & Amanda, 9/31/1865-10/26/1870, 5y2m26d
Brenbarger, Mary E., d/o John & Amanda, 10/14/1874-10/10/1878, 4y10d
Miller, Bertha, d/o Hiram & Amanda, 8/11/1893-8/8/1894
Miller, Minnie E., d/o Hiram & Amanda, 4/7-8/26/1885
Miller, Susan, d/o Hiram & Amanda, 8/13/1871-5/25/1885, 13y8m25d
Miller, Charlie E., s/o Hiram & Amanda, 9/1-21/1870, 20d
Miller, Walter C., s/o Hiram & Amanda, ar., 10/17/1888-10/19/1910
Miller, Hiram B., Co. K 187 Pa. Inf., 1848-1927
Miller, Amanda Coble, his w., 1850-1922
Cramer, Clarence, Pvt., 1st Cl. Col. 6th Line, WWI, 1895-1949
Cramer, Mabel E. Burkhart, w., 1897-1971
(C)
Reinhart, Frederick B., f., 8/21/1925-12/12/1960
Reinhart, Mary C., m., 10/12/1921-
Reinhart, Dennis A., s/o Frederick B. & Mary C., 6/24-26/1951, 2d
Micken, Mylin M., 4/23/1916-10/9/1969
Micken, Adalyne E. Reese, his w., 1/29/1919-8/19/1952
Heisler, Benita L. Micken, w., 11/22/1907-10/30/1953
Heisler, Alfred E., h., 2/8/1917

Row 18A
Snyder, Henry
Snyder, Adam

Row 19
Jones, Leora Mary, our baby, d/o Harry & Olive S.,6/22/1902-7/6/1903
___, Reba A., 7/29/1899-2/6/1900, 6m9d
___, Hambright, 3/24/1897-3/12/1898, 7m8d
___, Frankie, 9/15/1894-12/14/1896, 2y2m29d
Miles, Mary M., w/o Frank, m., 3/29/1832-3/2/1892
Miles, Frank, 20 Ohio Batt. 5/26/1912. GAR
2 field stones//W.H.H.//J.H.//B.H.//C.E.D.//A.D.
Kepperling, Henry, 9/28/1801-2/20/1882, 74y-m-d
McNeal, Jno., Co. D 120th Pa. Inf.
4 field stones
Unmarked [2]
Dyer, Benj. F., f., Pvt. Co. D 195, Pa. Inf. V, 5/23/1833-10/6/1911,
    78y4m13d
Dyer, Mary, w/o Benj. F., m., 12/7/1837-9/6/1887, 50y9m2d
Dyer, Charles A., s/o Benj. F. & Mary, 4/23/1875-
Dyer, Benton K., s/o Benj. F. & Mary, 1871___/29/1871, 9m11d
Dyer, William A., s/o Benj. F. & Mary, 1/20/1868-3/30/1871, 3y2m10d
Dyer, Mary E., d/o Benj. F. & Mary
Dyer, H. E., 1884-1932

Row 20
Coble, Harry, 1868-1931
Coble, Harriet E., his w., 1871-1945
Coble, Margaret S., d/o Harry & Harriet, 7/20/1895-4/11/1896
Coble, Anna M., d/o Harry & Harriet, 2/8/_7/11/1889
Coble, Harry N., s/o John & ___, d. 2/8/1890, 5m8d
Coble, Maggie R., d/o John & ___, d. 9/2/1881, 1y5m1d

Row 21
A.E.//E.E.//J.E.//M.A.E.//J.E.

COLEMANVILLE METHODIST CHURCH CEMETERY
Colemanville, Conestoga Township

Colemanville Methodist Church cemetery is across the street
(Colemanville Rd.) from this Church. Page 742 of Ellis & Evans, *History
of Lancaster Co., Pa.* states this church land was given by Mrs. Coleman
and that the church was built in 1849, members coming from the Mt.
Nebo Methodist Church, Martic Twp.

Coming from Lancaster go south on Prince St., taking right at the
Engleside Bridge onto New Danville Pike. Go thence to Rt. 324, turn left
and stay on road through Marticville, Martic Forge, over the bridge and
the second right turn is Colmanville Rd., going 2/10 of a mile the church
is on your right. The cemetery is at the corner of Colmanville Rd. and
Colemanville Church Road.

There are 24 rows; very few are full rows. This yard is well cared for, but
many tombstones are missing. I have been told that there were a few
slate tombstones at the top of the cemetery, but when this yard was
cleaned and reset - they straightened the rows and removed the broken
slate stones. The stone wall is on the front and left side, midway up
Colemanville Church Road. It is on a hill, slooping about 40-30 degrees
to the church.

The following were recorded from the bottom, walking up the hill.

Row 1
Lewis, Walter F., father, 1879-1904
Lewis, Edith H. Gainer, his w., mother,1882-1919

Row 2
Garrett, George, bro., 7/29/1831-3/10/1909, 77y7m11d
Garrett, Barbara, sis., 1/25/1834-8/4/1906, 72y6m9d

Wagner, Peter, f., d. 3/18/1909, GAR marker, 65y5m29d
Wagner, Mary A., m., d. 1/30/1932
Kone, Jesse D., f., 1/11/1880-10/28/1918
Palmer, Karl V., 1/24/1899-9/27/1948
Palmer, Ella, 5/16/1885-10/4/1958
Loveless, William A., husband, 1/13/1900-9/28/1845
Walter, Jacob, 1/5/1898-7/18/1903, 13y6m3d
Walter, George, 10/3/1891-7/18/1903, 12y3m5d
Walter, Frank W., 1866-1939
Walter, Adeline J., 1871-1950

Row 3
Sellers, Edward J., s/o Wm. H. & Annie E., 1900-1929
Musser, Ernest E., f., 9/8/1885-1/24/1977
Musser, Ethel Sellers, w/o Ernest E., m., 12/12/1888-1/14/1913, 24y1m2d
Gainer, William T., 1840-1918
Gainer, Elizabeth G., his w., 1844-1916
Rice, Frederick, 7/29/1880-6/9/1906, 26y
Rice, Maris, 1846-1890
Rice, Louisa C. Campbell, his wife, 1848-1926
Goss, Frank, s/o John & Ivie, 6/7/1927-11/18/1928
Goss, John, 1902-1974
Goss, Ivie, 1902-

Row 4
Sellers, George D., s/o Wm. H. & Annie E., 1899-1921
Sellers, Wm. H., 1870-1924
Sellers, Annie E., his w., 1879-1940
Sellers, Martha J., d/o WM. & Martha, 8/15/1868-7/17/1871
Sellers, William, f., GAR marker, 5/15/1842-4/3/1927, 68y11m15d
Sellers, Martha, m., 10/17/1843-1/18/1927, 83y2m21d
OUR BOYS, in memory of whose who met death in the explosion of
    dynamite 6/9/1906:
    Shoff, Phares R., 5/18/1888 - 6/9/1906
    Funk, Wm. S., 9/18/1886 - 6/9/1906
    Rinier, Benj. E., 10/12/1882 - 6/9/1906
    Rinier, Joseph H., 5/15/1888 - 6/9/1906
    Boatman, John W., 1/6/1888 - 6/9/1906
    Parker, Collin W., 3/11/1889 - 6/9/1906
    Turner, Ernest S., 8/16/1884 - 6/9/1906
    Hathaway, Gust. A., 5/19/1885 - 6/9/1906
    Myers, John G., 12/18/1857 - 6/9/1906
Ressler, Barbara, widow of Ephraim, m., 10/10/1826-3/31/1895, 68y5m21d
Harnish, ___, ch/o Joseph & Mary, d. 2/27/1890
Harnish, May Virginia, ch/o Joseph & Mary, 1888-1890

Harnish, Jessie Clay, ch/o Joseph & Mary, 1886-1889
Harnish, Joseph Clinger, ch/o Joseph & Mary, 10/6-10/1884
Harnish, infant son, ch/o Joseph & Mary, 10/26/1877

Row 5
Funk, Samuel R., f., Co. D 49th Pa., GAR, 3/3/1822-10/30/1904, 82y7m27d
Funk, Elizabeth, m., 10/7/1826-11/29/1901, 75y1m22d
Funk, Blair, 1860-1941
Funk, Anna M., his w., 1869-1922
Funk, Suie E., d/o Blair & Anna, 8/2/1891-9/31/1891
Funk, Bertha, d/o Blair & Anna, 3/9/1889-1/10/1906, 17y
LaVigne, Glenn, 8/18/1952-12/12/1952
LaVigne, Mary H., 4/7/1923-9/19/1967
LaVigne, Malcom E., 8/19/1920-
Clark, John G., f., 1871-1949
Clark, Mary F., m., 1892-1963
Garrett, Walter H., f., 1896-1943
Garrett, Marion Harnish, m., 1894-19__
Garrett, George K., f., 3/14/1858-3/1/1936
Garrett, S. Alice, m., 9/4/1860-6/19/1925

Row 6
Gardner, Nellie Senft, w/o John W., 5/14/1862-1/13/1936
Gardner, John, GAR, 2/14/1841-5/8/1924, 83y
Gardner, Henrietta C., w/o J. W., d. 12/28/1896, 66y
Sickman, Henry, f., GAR, Co. I 11th Pa. Cav., 4/1/__ -4/15/1909,
  74y5m18d
Sickman, Susan, m., w/o Henry, d. 2/1/1897, 54y3m17d
Rineer, Retta M., dau., 1903-1917
Rineer, Edward F., f., 1876-1904
Rineer, Rebecca, m., 1881-1958
Ramsey, Elijah McInyre, 1846-1886
Ramsey, Antaline Eshleman, 1851-1924
Ramsey, Cora Lucinda, 1875-1878
Ramsey, Irene R. Donovan, 1878-1965
Cramer, Charles, 1863-1939
Cramer, Mary L. Wise, his w., 1864-1910
Cramer, Walter, son, 1885-1886
Cramer, Carl E., s/o Clyde & Anna, d. 5/25/1922
Cramer, Clare M., d/o Clyde & Anna, d. 11/15/1927
Cramer, Clyde, 1890-1947
Cramer, Anna Eshleman, his w., 1889-1947

Row 7
Rineer, Aaron, husband, no date

Rineer, Emma, wife, no date
Senft, Solomon, f., 12/13/1819-9/22/1884, 65y9m9d
Senft, Sarah, m., 10/3/1825-1/16/1912
Senft, Edward, f., 12/28/1850-6/15/1917
Senft, Annie S., m., w/o Edward, 6/17/1851-9/16/1917
McCardle, Albert, f., 1847-1919

Row 8
Gardner, Catharine, d/o John & Leah, 4/14/1843-6/29/1865, 22y2m15d
Gardner, Valentine, s/o John & Leah, 10-15/1850-12/7/1871, 21y1m23d
Gardner, Mary, d/o John & Leah, d. 3/11/1836, 9 weeks
Gardner, Elizabeth, d/o John & Leah, d. 5/9/1837, 22d
Gardner, Joseph, s/o John & Leah, d. 12/26/1859, 11y6m5d
Gardner, Leah, d/o John & Leah, d. 2/28/1853, 14y10m20d
Gardner, Leah, m., w/o John, 9/19/1811-6/15/1886, 74y8m26d
Gardner, John, f., 10/16/1807-5/16/1894, 86y7m
Rice, William, f., 9/15/1804-10/27/1887, 83y1m12d
Rice, Martha, m., w/o William, 8/22/1813-3/10/1883, 69y6m19d
Rice, Frederick, GAR, 9/25/1840-3/26/1877, 36y6m1d
Senft, Fannie Z., d/o Howard & Mary, d. 2/23/1884/3m27d

Row 9
Shoff, Anna, m., w/o Christian, 9/12/1822-3/21/1899
Shoff, Christian, Sr., f., 12/27/1821-6/25/1905, 83y8m28d
Shoff, Elizabeth, m., w/o Christian, 3/28/1825-6/24/1868
Shoff, Franklin, s/o Christian & Eliza, no dates
Shoff, George, s/o Christian & Eliza, 4/5/1866-5/19/1881, 15y4d
White, Mary, w/o Rev. Henry & d/o Levi & Margt. Shenck, 8/1/1831-
    6/6/1875, 43y10m5d
Keller, Mary Virginia, d/o John H. & Eliz., 6/7/1870-11/9/1878, 8y6m2d
Hill, Nancy, w/o Frederick, d. 7/4/1898
Hill, Frederick, f., 1/31/1812-4/19/1882, 70y2m19d
Hill, Mary, d/o ___ & ___, 3/13-5/4/1877, 1m21d
Hill, Catharine, d/o Fredr. & Ann, 4/8/1838-7/10/1839
Hill, Anna M., d/o Andrew & Susan, 5/22/1873-10/11/1874
Hill, Andrew, GAR, 1844-1874
Bortzfield, Susan Hill, 1849-1946
Ressel, George W., bro., 8/1/1847-12/20/1924
Parker, H. Elizabeth, m., 1856-1923
Parker, William W., f., 1852-1940
Weitzel, Fannie P., m., 1877-1949
Weitzel, Charles E., 1877-1957
Lobb, Robert K., 1931-1975
Lobb, Patricia, 1935-
Houpt, Levi R., 10/11/1903-9/1/1976

Houpt, Margaretta, 8/5/1906-
Shertzer, John W., 1923-1976

Row 10
Wilhelm, Jacob, 12/24/1806-2/6/1870, 64y1m13d
Shenck, Rudalph, s/o Rudalph & Catha., 6/10/1810-5/19/1838, 27y11m19d
Shenk, Christian, s/o Christian & Anna, d. 5/29/1850, 76y9m8d
Shenk, Christian, d. 8/8/1833, 84y6m3d
Shenk, Anna, w/o Christian, d. 8/4/1821, 75y7m15d
Shenck, Mary Wesley, w/o Henry S., 11/24/1790-12/1/1861, 71y7d
Shenk, Henry, 4/11/1788-8/30/1868, 80y4m16d
Shenck, Elias, s/o Henry & Mary, 3/10/1813-4/30/1824, 11y1m20d
Shenck, Judith, d/o Henry & Mary, 7/23/1817-2/25/1823, 5y7m2d
Shenck, Rachel, d/o Henry & Mary, 3/12/1822-8/5/1822, 4m24d
Shenck, Jonas, s/o Rudalph & Catha., d. 10/2/1822, 40y9m10d
Keller, Martin J., our babe, 1883
Parker, Lizzie, w/o C.B., 1/27/1889-2/13/1913
Parker, Melvin W., Span.-Amer. War, 5/13/1872-7/9/1941
Parker, Rodger W., Sr., 1911-1979
Parker, Rodger W., Jr., 1947-1975
Parker, Ruth F., 1915-1961
Parker, Patsy Mae Sheltown, 1938-
Deets, John, 1812 War marker, no dates, 90y3m4d

Row 11
Lyons, infant son/o Wm. & Eliz.
Lyons, Lizzie, d/o Wm. & Eliz., 1869-1873, 3y
Hess, John G., f., 5/15/1864-1/11/1898, 58y7m26d
Hess, Martha A., m., 2/3/1838-9/8/1917, 79y7m5d
Reikard, Mary A., w/o John, 10/26/1810-11/23/1898
R.
W.R.
Armstrong, William F., f., 1870-1949
Armstrong, Ralph F., s., 1887-1919
Armstrong, Jennie R., m., 1867-1948
Herr, Lloyd G., 1884-1960
Herr, Barbara F., 1890-1951
Herr, Alma Mae, 1910-1936
Herr, B. Frank, 1/17/1914-11/25/1968
Warfel, Amos S., 1920
Warfel, Catharine, 1915-1972
Lasher, Paul W., 1927-1974
Hess, Edward L., 1895-
Hess, Elsie M., 1897-1976

Row 12
Laird, John, 1830-1918
Laird, Emma Jane, 1834-1905
McMellen, John, 5/4/1831-1/18/1895
McMellen, Martha J. A., 8/5/1833-8/22/1905
Boatman, Galen S., s/o Henry & Abbie, 11/201906-6/18/1907, 6m18d
Boatman, Florence, d/o Henry & Abbie, 2/27/1891-7/26/1892, 1y5m
Boatman, Jacob H., s/o Henry & Abbie, 8/13/1884-7/18/1897
Boatman, Nagma, d/o Henry & Abbie, 8/12/1905-7/28/1906, 11m16d
Wagner, George, 5/26/1838-12/22/1900, 62y6m26d
Wagner, Elizabeth, 8/27/1839-10/3/1905, 66y2m4d
Wagner, infant son, no dates
M.R.
Rinier, Martin V., f., 1858-1939
Rinier, Mary Alice, m., 1861-1941
Rinier, Reba V., 1903-1908
R.
Rinier, John M., f., 1/31/1870-12/18/1928
Rinier, Bertha C., m., his wife, 6/23/1870-5/18/1948
Rice, Franklin, 1872-1933
Rice, Barbara Warfel, his w., 1873-1955
Herr, Minnie, 6/4/1906-9/14/1952
Herr, Lester B., 12/5/1904-9/1/1974
Rampy, Beverly S. Kling, dau. 1950-1971
Lambert, George F., funeral marker, 1900-1976
Lambert, Dorothy H., funeral marker, 1901-1974
Rineer, Jesse, f., WWI, 1894-1975
Rineer, Catherine M., m., 1906-1974

Row 13
Ewing, Mary J., m., 3/4/1819-2/6/1886, 66y10m25d
Ewing, James A., f., 7/16/1819-1/1/1881, 61y3m26d
Babe
Massey, Louisa, 1861-1886
Massey, Lewis, 1860-1887
Boatman, Benjamin F., f., 3/24/1859-2/16/1889, 29y10m23d
Boatman, John W., f., 4/15/1830-8/31/1899, 69y4m16d
Boatman, Hannah, 1830-1912, 82y
footstone, no name or dates
Sellers, Daisy, m., 3/14/1884-4/28/1943
Sellers, John W., f., 12/2/1874-4/4/1934
Gochenaur, Adam F., f., 1857-1935
Gochenaur, Susan, m., 1865-1937
Gochenaur, Ralph B., s., Pvt. Co. L, 1th Inf., WWI, 2/5/1890-8/21/1973
Canada, Richard E., Jr., b./d. 6/5/1969

Sellers, Wm., f., 1903-1970
Sellers, Viola M., m., 1906-
Rankin, Lloyd J., 1936-1976
Rankin, Janet L., 1934-

Row 14
Gardner, Mary A., d/o Benj. & Catha., 12/21/1851-9/4.1856, 4y8m10d
Taylor, Martha, d/o Wm. J. & Julianna, d. 12/12/1856, 5y9m22d
Warfel, Levi W., 1860-1926
Warfel, Annie, his wife, 1862-1914
Warfel, Fredy D., s/o Levi & Annie, 9/1/1886-2/20/1895, 9y
McCardle, Mary, d/o Jospeh & Susan, 10/7/1842-12/3/1901
McCardle, Susan, w/o Joseph, 7/2/1818-7/7/1906, 88y5d
McCardle, Joseph, 9/30/1809-1/19/1875, 65y3m20d
Uffelmann, ___ Spar Den, Alt. 1 Tage (in German), d. 12 Sep 1856
Uffelmann, Anna Mary Charlotte Sparbden, Alt 8 Jahr, d. 30 Oct 1855
Gray, George S., GAR, 1864-1911
Myers, Annie Gray, 1869-1954
Harrison, Mary F., dau., 3/21/1896-2/4/1916
Herman, Sarah E., 1854-1922
Sellers, Harry H., s/o Harry & Cornelia, 6/11-8/25/1931
Wagner, Frederick, 1895-1947
Wagner, Laura E., 1890-1969
Wagner, Clarence C., 1930-
Frey, Marguerite S., 1917-1979
Frey, Amos F., 1914-1967
Frey, Walter M., Sgt. 444 A.F.B.U., 1921-1969
Frey, Katherine J., 1922-
Imhoff, Katherine J., 1922-
Imhoff, Charles B., WWII, 1910-
Morrison, Frank, f., WWI, 1899-1976
Morrison, Grace, m., 1900-1971
Frey, Clarence W., WWII marker, 8/20/1918-12/12/1971
Frey, Pauline R., 6/8/1919-

Row 15
Harnish, Mary, d/o Samuel & Delilah, 5/11/1840-1/13/1841
Harnish, Henry S., s/o Samuel & Delilah, 3/23/1844-9/4/1846, 2y5m12d
Harnish, Jonas, s/o Samuel & Delilah, d. 8/5/1854, 1y8m10d
Harnish, Delilah Ann, d/o Samuel & Delilah, d. 1/20/1864, 5y10m10d
Harnish, Milton W., s/o Samuel & Delilah, bro., 9/17/1846-7/20o/1876,
    29y10m3d
Harnish, Delilah, w/o Samuel, m., 12/16/1818-12/9/1876, 57y11m23d
Harnish, Prudence, d/o Samuel & Delilah, 9/14/1841-8/12/1889, 38y11m4d
Harnish, Samuel, f., 11/12/1816-3/5/1893

Bowers, William C., 1856-1929
Bowers, Catharine A., 1860-1938
Bowers, Catharine A., 12/31/1888-5/4/1959
Bowers, Thomas F., son, 2/12/1886-3/26/1970
Bowers, Thomas, Co. C 12 Pa. Vol., 6/18/1830-10/16/1899, 69y3m23d
Bowers, Hannah J., w/o Thomas, 1833-1888
Hess, George E., 1870-1930
Hess, Laura Bowers, his w., 1869-1917
L.B.//L.B.//C.B.//3 broken stones
Dattilo, Nancy, 1870-1923
Wagner, William F., 1870-1942
Wagner, Mary H., his w., 1862-1934
Wissler, John R., 1875-1942
Wissler, Anna Mary Bowers, his w., 1883-1966
Kleinhans, Carl S., f., PFC 6817th Special Serv. Batt., WWII, 2/29/1917-4/28/1966
Kleinhans, Fred, WWII, 1902-1967
Kleinhans, Florence, 1901-1973

Row 16
Clark, Henry, no dates
Clark, Emma C., 1860-1876
Clark, Jacob, f., d. 2/5/1900, 79y11m23d
Clark, Sarah, m., d. 11/24/1891, 77y8m4d
Clark, William, 1850-1896
Clark, Martha J., 1855-1927
Reikard, Wm., f., 10-7/1831-12/8/1906, 75y2m21d
Reikard, John, s/o Harriet, 3/17/1858-8/13/1868, 10y4m26d
___, rusting funeral marker
McClune, Susan, m., w/o Rawlins, 6/22/1836-9/5/1888, 52y2m13d
Hill, Joseph H., 1895-1920
Pribicevic, Paul, 4/10/1886-6/22/1964
Pribicevic, Mildred, w/o Paul, 8/27/1885-6/27/1926
Pribicevic, Anna E., 9/25/1910-3/19/1931
Hill, Helen V., 1921-1967

Row 17
Trafford, Mary F., 6/8/1830-9/29/1852, 22y3m12d
Wise, Frederick, 10/21/1838-11/19/1911, 73y23d
Foreman, Joseph L., 6/22/1879-9/28/1904
Foreman, Clara J., d/o Thomas & Fanny, 8/30/1877-9/25/1878
Foreman, Thomas Dungan, 1849-1881
Foreman, Fannie Beach, his w., 1850-1930
Funk, William, f., 10/29/1866-8/6/1913
Funk, Lloyd, s., 1/15/1902-10/7/1921

Hake, Gerard E., WWII, funeral marker, 1890-1950
Gebhart, Chester K., 1898-1946
Gebhart, Wilhelmein, 1908-
Fitzkel, Mabel M., m., 2/27/1896-12/1/1960
Osborne, Nettie B., funeral marker, 1888-1966
Huber, Kathleen Harkins, wife, 12/15/1940-7/8/1970

Row 18
Lugren, Mary A., 1864-1904
Lugren, James T., 1865-1942
Lugren, Walter F., Jr., s/o Walter & Nancy, Vietnam conflict, 7/24/1957-7/31/1977
Bowers, Reba, d/o J. Walter & Martha H., b./d. 2/22/1910
Bowers, Martha H., m., 5/26/1883-10/12/1938
Bowers, J. Walter, f., 12/9/1880-9/13/1921
Peters, Kate, wife, 1860-1928
Peters, Samuel H., husband, 1856-1928
Gemmill, John A., f., 1863-1938
Gemmill, Mary (M.), 1863-1937
Claycomb, Mary, m., 1/19/1899-1/14/1920
Unsworth, Edna M., 10/24/1887-5/12/1912
Eppeheimer, Edward J., 1/25/1848-1/31/1920, 72y
Eppeheimer, Susan, w/o Edward J., 12/7/1856-6/2/1910, 53y
Eppeheimer, Samuel S., bro., 12/1/1884-9/15/1921, 39y
Neil, Robert B., s/o Fitzhugh & Ida, 8/13/1915-5/10/1916
Neil, Ida I., m., 1894-1957
Neil, Fitzhugh, 1891-1947
Neil, James E., 1862-1947
Neil, Alice M., his w., 1871-1926
Neil, Curtis, son, 1889-1925
Smith, Maris K., 1897-1979
Smith, Edna M., 1899-1931
Neill, John E., 1888-1967
Monaghan, William H., 1871-1937
Monaghan, Eliz. M., m., 1877-1961
Eppeleimer, Edward J., bro., 1882-1938
Wagner, Richard C., WWII, 1923-1978
Wagner, Thomas Bruce, s/o Richard E. & Kathryn, 1954-
Morrison, Kenneth G., s/o Glenn R. & Flora M., 7/26/1949-1/25/1962
Reihart, Anna J., wife, m. 11/24/1915, 1894-1970
Reihart, Henry, 1895-1963
Buckwalter, Clayton Herr, f., 11/9/1915-
Buckwalter, Erma Eshleman, m., 12/1/1918-11/5/1924

Row 19
Wagner, Helen L., d/o Lawrence & Mary M., 10/18/1917-10/22/1918
Wagner, Mary M., w/o Lawrence, 10/26/1897-2/14/1922
Lungren, Paul, s/o Mary E. & Paul E.
Lungren, Mary E., 11/7/1900-5/__/1973
Lungren, Paul E., 11/9/1902-
Boatman, Charles L., 7/16/1912-5/16/1943
Boatman, Lloyd C., 1883-1967
Boatman, Anna E., m., 1883-1941
Boatman, Harry C., f., 1860-1938
Boatman, Abbie Jane Bleacher, his w., m., 1861-1935
Gingher, Alfred B., infant s/o Alfred & Matilda, 9/13-15/1910
Gingher, Alfred B., 1890-1944
Gingher, Matilda J., 1890-
Beach, Etta L., w/o John W., 2/20/1874-7/29/1910

1/2 way between row 19 & 20 is 1 stone:
Douts, Phillip Gordon, 4/25/1949-1/25/1951
Rinier, Joseph G., Co. C 135th Pa. Inf., 1925-
Rineer, J. Westley, 1891-1952
Rineer, Matilda E., 1892-
Rineer, Mildred M., d/o J. W. & Matilda, 12/7/1930-5/18/1931
Ewing, Carl J., WWI, f., 1888-1959
Ewing, Mary R., m., 1861-1935
Ewing, James S., f., 1860-1934
___, Susan E., dau., 1947-1949
Sellers, Richard W. & Laraine, infant twins, d. 1942
Good, Nora W., 11/15/1876-10/1/1954
Good, Oliver, 5/6/1876-1/26/1973
___, funeral marker, no name
Johnson, Nellie S., 8/25/1889-1/31/1974
Kelly, Clara A., 8/2/1884-10/27/1974
Kelly, L. Burns, 7/14/1910-6/1/1961
Gardner, Edmond, 1870-1957
Gardner, Mary Miller, his w., 1872-1960
Gardner, Grace, 1896-
Gardner, Clare H., 1898-
Gardner, John Harold, 1894-1970
Gardner, Sarah Dempsey, his w.
___, funeral marker, no name
Cauler, William L. J., 1904-1972
Cauler, Anna E., m., 1909-1972

Row 20
Lanious, Aaron R., s/o Chester & Isabella, 3/3-4/17/1917

Lanious, John S., s/o Chester & Isabella, 3/3-4/8/1917
Lanious, Helen E., d/o Chester & Isabella, 6/8/1915-1/13/1916
Lanious, Chester R., 1892-1952
Lanious, Isabella L., 1893-1972
Lanious, Horace P., WWII, killed in Germany, 1924-1944
Reikard, Leah M., d/o Howard & Rebecca, 3/14/1910-9/12/1917
Katz, Pearl E., m., 1910-1943
Shertzer, Ray L., WWI, 8/21/1908-9/19/1939
Shertzer, Mary H., 6/16/1901-7/15/1963
Shertzer, Robert L., 2/23/1925-3/30/1974
Weidler, Aaron G., 11/6/1893-6/6/1959
Weidler, Phillip Gordon, s/o Gordon & Hilda, 1942-1943
Warfel, Andrew, 1847-1925
Warfel, Alice, his w., 1855-1952
Kleinhans, Frederick L, 1874-1945
Kleinhans, Cora B. Sickman, 1880-1951
Kleinhans, Claude S., WWII, 1918-1959
Kleinhans, Robert M., Pvt. C. K 23 Inf., 2 Div., 2 Army, Killed at
    Normandy, 1922-1944
Kleinhans, Harry, f., 1898-1957
Kleinhans, Lena, m., 1900-1977
Eshleman, Dawn Marie, d/o Brt. & Freda K., b./d. 10/3/1949
Reikard, Lloyd Sr., WWI, 1900-1966
Pries, Earl W., 1885-1975
Pries, Sus H., 1883-1971
Parker, Harry N., 1890-1968
Parker, Mary E., m., 1892-1964
Ferguson, ___, WWII, USA, 5/23/1920-7/7/1965

Row 21
Saber, May L., d/o William & Virginia, 2/12/1922-5/18/1923
Garrett, Robert H., Jr., 12/27/1952-12/20/1958
___, new grave, no marker
Bortzfield, William, 1887-
Bortzfield, Jessie E., 1885-1970
Kleinhans, Paul, Jr., 1937-1960
Rinier, Charles A., 1886-1963
Rinier, Ruth May, 1898-

Row 22
Wagner, Jesse E., 1866-1936
Wagner, Eliz. E., 1864-1944
Henry, Willis P., 10/26/1915-10/19/1944
Stamm, David P., 1880-1947
Stamm, Eliz. R. Titzel, his w., 1878-1965

Richmond, Harry, Jr., 6/1/1904-9/3/1950
Richmond, Arlean, 3/31/1904-
Whitmyer, Charles Westley, d. 5/30/1950
Whitmyer, Nettie A., d. 1/6/1951
Shoff, Fred Jr., 1895-1952
Shoff, Mary, 1894-1974
Warfel, Cora M., m., 1881-1952
Warfel, Albert D., f., 1879-1965
Warfel, William R., 10/8/1901-6/23/1966
Warfel, Myrtle, 2/13/1898-8/1/1971
Funk, Edmond, 2/23/1893-10/10/1972
Funk, Lillie J., 6/22/1895-2/5/1976
Brady, Ethel M., dau., 1/24/1929-5/15/1952
Becker, Myrtle, m., 1900-1971
Newport, Violet, funeral marker, 1904-1978
Carrington, Charles R., 1889-1957
Carrington, Bertha Rinier, w., 1898-1967
Boatman, Maris, WWI, 1896-1972
Arnold, Joseph C., 1895-
Arnold, Katherine M., 1896-1968
Rankin, Scotty, our son, d. 8/14/1960, 2m
Busswood, Frederick T., 1904-1966
Busswood, Frances M., 1905-

Row 23
Koch, Darrell, funeral marker, 1909-1977
Erb, George F., 12/25/1916-
Erb, Gladys V., 10/9/1919-11/24/1976
Welk, Lisa M., d/o Kenneth & Joan, 1/3/1969-1/8/1978
Warfel, Marion G., WWII, 1/19/1922-1/24/1977
Warfel, Gladys N., 6/12/1925-
Greenawalt, Jeffrey H., 2/14/1962-9/1/1978

Row 24
Weaver, Robert W., 10/9/1927-7/20/1977
Weaver, Pearl E., 7/27/1930-
Wagner, Berl W., 1913-1978

Appendix A: VETERANS BURIED IN MARTIC TOWNSHIP

REVOLUTIONARY WAR
Schweicker, Sebr.

WAR OF 1812
Deets, John
Pfeiffer, Fredr.
Sweigart, Felix

MEXICAN-AMERICAN WAR
Parker, Edward F.

CIVIL WAR
_ell, Aug. C., GAR
Alexander, Maris, Co. K, 77 Pa. Vol.
Armstrong, Henry, Co. E, 1st Pa. Rev.
Armstrong, Hugh, GAR
Barton, John H., h., Co. E 79th Rgt. Pa. Vol.
Bleacher, Martin, Co. H, 79th Pa. Vol.
Bowers, Thomas, Co. C 12 Pa. Vol.
Brooks, Henry S., Co. K 203 Pa. Vol.
Brubaker, Benj., Co. K, 2nd Pa. Cav.
Brubaker, Benj., Co. E, 2nd Pa. Cav., GAR
Brubaker, Wm., GAR
Burns, John, Col. H., 203d Pa. Ind.
Campbell, Geo., GAR
Campbell, Hiram, GAR
Campbell, J., Co. _, 79th Pa. Inf.
Carrigan, Hiram, GAR
Clark, Brice, Co. H, 79 Pa.
Clark, Joseph, GAR
Conway, John, Co. H., 203d Pa. Ind.
Cramer, Amos, 1st Lt. Co. B 99 Rgt. PVI
Cramer, Daniel, Col. K., 79th Pa. Vol.
Cramer, James, GAR
Cramer, John C., Co. B 7 Rgt. PV Cav.
Cramer, John C., Co. B, 79 Pa. Cav.
Cramer, Phillip, Co. D, 2nd Pa. Cav.
Crawford, John, Co. K, 50 Pa.
Crawford, Theo., _-1872, GAR
Creamer, Hiram L., Corp., s/o - & -, GAR
Cummings, Tom, Co. H, 122 Pa.
Douglass, Rbt., Co. A, 9th NJ
Douglass, Samuel, Co. K 181 D Cav.

Drumm, George W., GAR
Drumm, Isaac, Co. B 78 Rgt. Ohio Vol., GAR
Drumm, Samuel, Co. H. 79th Rgt. Pa. Vol., GAR
Drumm, Wm. Urie, s/o Peter & Eliz., Vol. Co. D 2 Regt. Pa.
Duke, John R., GAR
Eshleman, Calvin, GAR
Eshleman, Samuel, GAR
Eshleman, Samuel, GAR
Finefrock, Tobias, Rev., GAR
Fisher, Albert, GAR
Fisher, Fredr., Co. B, 1st Md.
Fisher, Fredrick B., Co. B 1st Md Lt. Art.
Fisher, John, GAR, Pa. Cav.
Flawd, David, Co. D 59 Rgt. Pvt., GAR
Folkman, Christian, GAR
Fullerton, J. A., Co. I, 20 Pa. Cav.
Funk, Michael, Co. D, 2nd Pa. Cav.
Funk, Samuel R., Co. D 49th Pa., GAR
Gardner, John, GAR
Gochnauer, Jacob, h., GAR
Good, Henry d., Co. I, 11th Pa. Cav.
Heeps, Henry, Co. H 203 Regt. PV
Heiney, George, Co. H., 203 Pa. Inf.
Heiney, George, Co. D, 1st Pa. Res.
Heiney, Isaac, Co. F, 9th Pa. Cav.
Heisler, Hiram, GAR
Hemperly, Alex., GAR
Herr, John, Co. K, 203 Pa. Vol.
Herr, Levi, Co. G., 79th Pa. Vol.
Hickey, Leo, Co. -- 5th Pa.
Himes, Wm., Co. M, 7th Pa. Cav.
Inf.,   re-en. Co. G 21 Regt. Pa. Cav.
Keffer, William A., d. in Mil. Hosp., GAR
Kepperley, John, Co. D 9th Pa. Cav.
Kirkwood, Thomas G., GAR
Kleinhaus, A., GAR
Kobel, Martin, Co. I 195th Rgt. Pa. Vol.
Kuhns, John, Co. O 91st Mass. Inf., GAR
Lehman, Jacob S., GAR
Locke, Abraham, GAR
McCardle, Samuel, Co. D, 195th Pa. Vol.
McClune, Lindey, GAR
McCombs, Amos, Co. C 20th Pa. Cav., GAR
McCombs, Harry, GAR
McCombs, Thom., Co. K 20th Pa. Cav.

McCue, James, GAR
McNeal, Jno., Co. D 120th Pa. Inf.
MeHaffey, James, GAR
Micken, Chas., Co. H 2nd Pa. Cav.
Miller, S., Co. I 7th Pa. Cav.
Moore, Samuel, Co. D 122 Pa., GAR
Morton, Benj., Co. D, 2nd Pa. Cav.
Null, Emory T., Co. D 2nd Rgt. Pa. Cav.
Nult, Leonard, 201st Pa. Inf. USA, flag
Oldham, H., GAR
Oldham, Jas., GAR, Pa. Art.
Plank, John J., GAR
Reese, Albert, Co. H 79th Pa. Inf., GAR
Rhoads, Jacob, Co. K 10 Regt. Pa. Vol. Inf., GAR
Rice, Frederick, GAR
Rice, John, Co. H, 11 Pa.
Rinier, Joseph G., Co. C 135th Pa. Inf.
Sellers, William, GAR marker
Shank, David, Pvt., Hebble's Pa. Cav.
Shoff, Felix, GAR, Pa. Batt.
Shoff, Henry, GAR
Sickman, Henry, GAR, Co. I 11th Pa. Cav.
Sowers, Conrad, GAR
Stephens, T. M., Co. K 5th Md. Inf.
Stevenson, S. C., GAR
Thomas, Albert, Co. I 64th Regt. Ohio Vol. Inf.
Thompson, Hiram L., Co. I, 122 Pa. Vol, GAR
Trimble, Thomas J., Co. G 21st Pa. Cav., Co. D 122 Inf.
Uffleman, Wm., Co. D, 122 Pa. Inf.
Urban, Benjamin F., Co. __, 79th Regt. P.I.V., in Goldsboro, NC, d.
Wagner, Peter, GAR marker, 65y5m29d
Weidhich, Ernest, GAR
White, James, GAR
Wiggins, Clayton, Pvt. Co. K 195th R., PV
Yingling, Geo.

SPANISH - AMERICAN WAR
Cramer, Edwin R., Co. K 7th Inf.
Cramer, Milton R.
Parker, Melvin W.

WORLD WAR I
Andre, John A.
Armstrong, Benj. F.
Boatman, Maris

Clark, Thaddeus J., Co. D 364 Eng. Div.
Cramer, Clarence, Pvt., 1st Cl. Col. 6th Line
Drumm, John R., Lt. Col. Army Air Corp.
Ewing, Carl J.
Feiler, John
Folkman, Wm., Pvt. USMC
Gochenaur, Ralph B., Pvt. Co. L, 1th Inf.
Holshouse, Peter, Q.M. Sgt. Co. I 20 Pa. Cav.
Landis, Samuel, Troop E, 11th Cav.
McCauley, Jasper W., Sgt. 23rd Field Hosp. US Army
McClune, I. Paul
Moore, Hartman
Morrison, Frank
Myers, Jacob, 304th Engr.
Nixdorf, Laird, Co. D, 111th Inf., 28 Div.
Oldham, Charles, USMC
Priest, Ira H., Cpl.
Quade, Elmer
Reikard, Lloyd Sr.
Rineer, Jesse
Shertzer, Ray L.
Shiffer, John E.
Shiffer, John
Wiederrecht, Lloyd G., Pvt. Co. C 30th Inf.

WORLD WAR II
Alexander, William H. P., US Navy
Alexander, Wm., US Navy
Baer, George H.
Bard, Charles, Navy
Beach, John H., US Navy
Clements, H. Gerald, Sgt. 6th Ord. Med. Maint. Co.
Dunn, Rbt. Eddie, Cpl., USAF
Ferguson, ___, USA
Frey, Clarence W.
Frey, Walter M., Sgt. 444 A.F.B.U.
Frownfelter, Wm. C., t/sgt/035 bomb qrp
Frownfelter, Wm., 35AF
Greene, Geo. E., QM T.C.
Greene, George E., 1906-1960
Hake, Gerard E.
Harner, Marvin, Co. I 4th Infantry Division
Heeps, Wm. H. Jr., 69th Div.
Imhoff, Charles B.
Kleinhans, Carl S., PFC 6817th Special Serv. Batt.

Kleinhans, Claude S.
Kleinhans, Fred
Kleinhans, Robert M., Pvt. C. K 23 Inf., 2 Div., 2 Army, Killed at Normandy
Lanious, Horace P., killed in Germany
LeFever, Arthur E., seaman 2nd GL
Loump, Dale E., s., 896 Anti Aircraft
Shaub, Benj. C., Sgt., Co. F 502nd Para. Inf. 101st Div., died in Holland
Shaubach, James S.
Shaubach, James
Shultz, David
Sigman, W. James, Pvt. 151st Machine Gun Bn.
Sigman, William James, Jr., US Marine Corp.
Wagner, Richard C.
Warfel, Marion G.
Winters, I. Clayre, Lt. Navy Nurse Corp
Wiggins, Ross, Jr.

KOREAN WAR
Labezius, Robert Donald, Korean War

VIETNAM WAR
Lugren, Walter F., Jr., s/o Walter & Nancy

UNKNOWN
Kilburn, Lenard, __ - 1947, Coxswain, US Navy

INDEX

44; Horace O., 44; I. Lucile
Hendricks, 57; Thomas E., 57
And---, Henry, 36; Meigart, 36;
Mary, 36
Andeus, Henry, 36; John Emory,
36; Meigart, 36
Andre, John A., 15, 103; Ruth L.,
15
Appel, Charlotte R., 5; Elwood S.,
5; Harry S., 16; James A., 16;
John, 16; Mary E., 16
Appleton, Annie, 64; Blanche, 64;
Ellie E., 64; Harriet, 36; Helen
W., 64; Henry, 36; John, 80;
John B., 56; John C., 64; Maris
L., 64; Mary S., 56; Mildred,
64; Myrtle Witmer, 64; Sarah,
36; William E., 64; William M.,
64
Arbaugh, Clarence P., 25; Philip,
25
Armstrong, Aldus E., 66; Anna
M., 45; Annie, 34; Annie M., 34;
Annie S., 34; B. Mildred, 45; B.
Mildred Russler, 45; Barbara
A., 50; Barbara A. Stokes, 37;
Benjamin F., 86, 103; Chester
A., 79; Christian H., 36; Clara,
51; Clarence F., 34; Clarence
William, 45; Daisey, 77; Daniel,
51; Daniel O., 57; E. Marion,
46; Elizabeth, 77; Elsie Clayre,
45; Elsie E., 86; F. Myrl, 37;
Fanny, 30; Grace, 77; H. Oliver,
37; Hannah, 30; Harold R., 37;
Hattie S., 57; Henrietta, 36;
Henry, 101; Howard H., 58;
Hugh, 30, 50, 101; James N.,
57; Jane, 30; Jane Ann, 30;
Jasper B., 37; Jennie R., 93;
John, 30; John A., 30; John K.,

79; John Robert, 86; Joseph,
30; Josephine, 51; Lottie, 79;
M. Wifield, 79; Martha J., 37;
Mary E., 79; Mary Edith, 34;
Myrtle, 34; Myrtle, 51; Oliver,
37; Paul, 37; Pauline, 37; Ralph
C., 45; Ralph F., 93; Ralph G.,
37; Ruthana, 45; S. Gordon, 50;
Susan, 37; Susan E. McMillen,
37; T. Jefferson, 77; Thomas,
34; William A., 93; William H.,
46; Willis S., 37
Arnold, Joseph C., 100;
Katherine M., 100
Aston, Amos K., 15; Barbara, 14;
Barbara E., 15; John D., 15;
Raymond Victor, 14; Walter W.,
15
Atkins, James, 29; Mary, 29

-B-

Bader, Ada Flowers, 27
Baer, George H., 12, 104;
Kathryn S., 12
Bair, Emma, 86; John, 86; Susan,
86
Baker, Catherine E., 22; Edward
O., 22
Ballantyne, Elizabeth Jardine, 56;
James, 56; Jean McLennan, 56;
Jessie L., 56; William M. H., 56
Ban, infant, 56; James, 56; Mary,
56
Barbon, Evelyn May, 10; Russel
L., 10
Barclay, Adaline M., 47; Allison,
48; Anna Myrtle, 46; Charles,
52, 53; Charles S., 53; Ellie N.,
46; Eva J., 52, 53; Helen
Shaub, 48; infant, 52, 53;
James F., 47; John, 48; John

Brady, Ethel M., 100; Frederick,
5
Brechbill, Clare Heisler, 77;
Laban T., 77
Brecjbill, Anna Ruth, 68; Carol
Jane, 68; H. Melvin, 68
Brenbarger, Amanda, 88;
Edward, 88; John, 88; Mary E.,
88
Brenberger, George M., 64;
Harry Martin, 65; Mary E.
Heeps, 65
Breneman, 20
Brenneman, ---lman, 85; Barbara,
22, 74; Benjamin S., 74;
Catharine, 77; Christian, 77;
John, 77; Mary Emma, 85;
Su---, 85
Brimmer, Amie Marguerite, 46;
Blanche C., 46; Lloyd S., 46
Brockway, Henry G., 6; Kate, 6
Brooks, A., 7; Alice L., 7; Anna,
6; Benjamin E., 7; Bertram N.,
20; Charles A., 6; Christian, 6;
Christian H., 11; Christiana K.,
6; Clara Minnie, 6; Elsie N.
Sterneman, 11; Harry E., 18;
Helen E., 7; Henry, 5; Henry
S., 6, 101; I. H., 7; I. Harvey, 7;
Ira M., 7; Jacob, 6; Mary, 6;
Mary A., 6; Mary E., 7; Miriam
May, 7; Orie E., 18; Pauline M.,
20; William, 6; William H., 6
Brown, Fanny, 51; Francis M.,
37; James, 3; Margaret A., 70;
Mary Emma, 37
Brubaker, Adaline, 51; Annie E.,
50; Argus, 27; Arthur C., 52;
Asa E., 49; Barbara, 11;
Benjamin, 27, 29, 101; Bertram
E., 52; Clara E., 50; Clarence

D., 49; Clayton I., 66; Cletus E.,
52; Delia, 50; E. Elmira, 50; E.
H., 24; Elizabeth, 27; Elmer E.,
50; Emanuel, 50; Emma H., 24;
Esther Ann, 50; Fannie J., 52;
Flora L., 49; G. Reed, 49;
George I., 44; George W., 50;
Goldie V., 52; Harry T., 52;
Herbert L., 50; J. T., 24; John,
24; John S., 27; Laura W., 66;
Lena Dorsey, 50; Lottie, 50;
Marie R., 52; Martha, 27; Mary
J. Stewart, 28; Mary M., 44;
Rolandus, 28; Theodore, 66;
William, 50, 101; William H., 51
Bruce, Amos F., 65; Earl Victor,
65; John, 74; Laura, 65; Mary,
74
Buchanan, John, 43; Margaret,
43
Buckwalter, Clayton Herr, 97;
Emma Eshleman, 97
Buffington, Mary, 25
Burkey, Eleanor M., 68
Burns, C., 3; Daniel, 3; Elizabeth,
3; Harriet C., 3; Hettie, 3;
John, 101; R., 3; Rebecca, 3;
Robert, 2; W., 3; William, 3
Bush, Mary A., 74
Bushum, Sarah Ann, 23; William,
18
Busswood, Frances M., 100;
Frederick T., 100
Byers, Emma L., 9; Harry T., 9;
Henry S., 9; Jacob, 6; Martha,
6

-C-
Camp, Grace, 34; Jennie, 34; W.
A., 34
Campbell, Andrew A., 39; Anna

102; Samuel G., 48; Samuel H., 69; Sarah, 41; Sarah A., 40; Susan Jenkins, 27; William Urie, 85, 102

Duffy, Agnes, 61; Albert, 62; Charles H., 61; Edwin L., 61; Frank, 61; James, 61; James B., 62; John, 61; Leah Ann, 61; Mary M., 61; Raymond, 61; Viola E., 62

Duke, John R., 71, 102

Duncan, James, 3; William, 3

Dunkle, A. S., 24; A. Stanley, 24; Annie H., 24; B. Cookman, 48; Clyde A., 44; Erma G., 44; George W., 45; Helen M., 24; J. B., 45; J. Benton, 45; J. Elmer, 44; James, 1; John, 45; John E., 24; John O., 44; Lilian, 45; Margaret I., 45; Marietta, 45; Mary, 45; Mary Alice Shoemaker, 48; Mary Spence, 45; Rebecca M., 45; Sue K., 44; Willie, 45

Dunn, Eddie R., 12; Robert Eddie, 13, 104; Winifred H., 12

Dyer, Benjamin F., 88; Benton K., 88; Charles A., 88; H. E., 88; Mary, 88; Mary E., 88; Willliam A., 88

-E-

Eberle, Amos H., 85; Dora Rineer, 85; Henry F., 51; Lona, 51

Ecklin, Antha Letitia, 43; Cora E., 44; David K., 43; Harry W., 44; James, 43; James F., 44; Jane, 43; John, 43; Joseph D., 43; L. A., 43; Martha, 43; Mary N., 44

Eckman, Albert, 74; Aldus J., 84; Charles J., 84; Clara P., 82; Clarence E., 87; Elizabeth, 76; Ella J., 84; Emma, 84; Emmanuel G., 51; Elsie J., 45; Esther M., 87; Fannie E., 74; George H., 53; Henry, 76; Hiram, 53, 54; infant, 53; John, 55; Joseph W., 84; Lizzie, 53; Mahlon P., 55; Margaret J., 55; Martha Broslet, 45; Mary M., 53; Ralph, 51, 53; Sallie E., 51; Sarah, 53; Sarah M., 54; Susan, 55; Walter, 82

Eisenberger, Abram, 43; Catharine, 85; Charles L., 82; Charles M., 78; Elam, 78; George W., 85; Harry Clinton, 85; Jacob, 85; Katherine M., 82; Maris, 43; Maris S., 82; Regina, 43; Samuel F., 85; Sarah, 43; Susan, 78

Elliott, Anna Lettie, 72; Benjamin F., 72; Benjamin H., 72; Emmet, 72; Fleming, 72; George, 72; George W., 72; I., 72; Isabella W., 72; John, 72; M., 72; Marian, 72; Mary, 72; Mifflin E., 72

Elmire, Irene M., 5

Engles, Benjamin L., 28; Jesse Oblando, 28; Joseph, 28; Mary, 28; Sarah E., 28

Eppeheimer, Edward J., 97; Samuel S., 97; Susan, 97

Eppeleimer, Edward J., 97

Erb, Ada A., 40; Agnes N., 32; Albert A., 60; Albert E., 27; Aldus E., 26; Alduse, 26; Alice H., 27; Amaziah W., 26; Amer. C., 33; Amos, 24; Amos E., 37;

S., 64; John H., 63; Margie R., 64

Farmer, Betty, 48; Frances S., 13; Harry H., 60; John C., 39; Kathryn E., 39; Marion A., 68; Mary S., 13; Minnie M., 60

Fehl, Aaron, 17; David, 5, 17; David W., 7; Eliza J. Wilson, 60; Esther, 17; George W., 17; Hannah, 17; Hannah W., 17; Henry P., 17; Jacob, 7, 17; Jacob W., 6; Sabena, 17; Susan, 7

Feiler, Amalia, 54; Daisy, 48; Daisy Frey, 48; Dennis, 48; Dorothea, 54; Glenn, 48; Glenn B., 48; Henry P., 47; infant, 54; John, 54, 104; John C., 54; John G., 54; Mollie, 54; Regie, 53; Rita Jean, 47; Sara M., 47; Sarah E., 47

Fellenbaum, Clyde S., 8; Estella M., 8

Ferguson, ---, 99, 104; William, 53

Figueroa, Ana, 68; Rosa, 68

Finefrock, Albert F., 87; Effie K., 87; Elmira, 81; Franklin G., 74; Harry P., 74; John, 87; L., 74; Mary, 87; Peter, 87; Susan, 87; Tobias, 81, 102

Fisher, Albert, 102; Albert J., 36; Anna Myers, 65; Annie M., 66; Dora M., 71; Frederick, 102; Frederick B., 65, 102; John, 56, 102; Orceneth Whitney, 11

Fitzkel, Mabel M., 97

Flawd, David, 78, 102; Elizabeth, 78

Flory, Paul Bowman, 41

Folkman, Catharine, 10; Charles, 12; Christian, 10, 102; Christian

B., 12; John G., 10; William, 10, 104

Foltz, Jacob, 52

Foote, Alice Harner, 45; Eleanor Carol, 45; Lawrence A., 45

Ford, Mary A. Groff, 70

Foreman, Clara J., 96; Fannie Beach, 96; Fanny, 96; Joseph L., 96; Thomas, 96; Thomas Dungan, 96

Foutz, Miller M., 15

Franklin, Ella L. Engle, 28

Frantz, Claire, 1

Frazer, David, 3; Margaret, 3

Frey, Amos F., 95; Clarence W., 95, 104; Katherine J., 95; Marguerite S., 95; Pauline R., 95; Walter M., 95, 104

Fritz, E. Helanie, 87; Norman A., 87; William, 87

Frownfelter, William, 104; William C., 58, 104

Fry, Mary V. Erb, 11

Fryberger, John H., 17

Frymyer, William S., 40

Fullerton, J. A., 32, 102

Fulton, Ann, 30; Anna S., 64; Fanny, 30; Henry, 30; John, 30; Raymond P., 64

Funk, Anna M., 91; Bertha, 91; Blair, 91; Dorothy M., 56; Edmond, 100; Elizabeth, 56, 91; Lillie J., 100; Lloyd, 96; Martin A., 65; Michael, 32, 102; Myrtle, 65; Ray A., 65; Ray E., 65; Samuel, 102; Samuel R., 91; Suie E., 91; Theodore R., 65; Thomas, 56; William, 96; William S., 90

-G-

E., 23; Hettie M., 11; infant, 14, 16, 23; Jacob, 22; Jacob K., 16; Johan, 22, 23; Johannes, 22; John, 16, 22, 23; John J., 16; John K., 23; John Sherman, 16; Jonas, 16; Jonas B., 9; Joseph, 16, 23; Joseph H., 16; Lizzie Urban, 11; Lloyd L., 14; Margaret, 5, 22; Maris, 19; Maris M., 16; Martha, 14; Martin H., 14; Mary, 16; Mary E., 14; Mary H., 16; Nora W., 98; Oliver, 98; Peter, 5, 22; Prudens, 22; S., 23; Susan, 23; Susan E., 23; Thaddus D., 16; Veronica, 16

Goss, Frank, 90; Ivie, 90; John, 90

Graham, William B., 66

Graman, Francina, 60

Graver, Chester H., 57; Mary W., 57; Shaun Douglas, 57

Gray, George S., 95; Hugh, 3

Graybill, Charles P., 49; Florence E. Drumm, 41; Mary E., 49; Raymond H., 41

Grebell, 23; Anna, 23; Jacob, 23

Greenawalt, Jeffrey H., 100

Greene, George E., 68, 104

Greis, Christian, 54

Greist, Isaac, 35; Margaret Ankrim, 35

Griffith, Albert, 63; Chester, 63

Grimsey, Charles G., 56; Clara E., 56; Elizabeth A., 56; Grace A., 56; William H., 56

Groff, baby boy, 20; Benjamin, 71; Benjamin F., 70; Benjamin M., 71; Clara Marinda, 47; Daniel, 39; Esther L., 71; F. B., 47; Frances, 68; Francis B., 47;

Frank, 71; Margaret M., 40; Maria, 47; Martha Miller, 71; Mary, 71; Myron D., 69; Samuel, 47; Willis K., 68

Gross, Ellen M., 87; William C., 87

-H-

Hackman, Benjamin F., 64; Christian, 64; Elizabeth, 64; Jacob, 64; John M., 64; Susan A., 64

Hagen, 36, 57; Angeline Heeps, 61; David, 26; Davis, 61; Davis H., 26; Elijah, 30; Emma C., 62; John, 62; Joshua, 30; Kate B., 38 Margaret M., 26; Mary, 30; Mary Jane, 36; Sarah, 30

Hake, Gerard E., 97, 104

Hambleton, B. Kinsey, 33; Emma C., 33; Mary E., 49

Hamil, Clayton W., 53; Mary M., 53

Hammond, Ann, 53; Thomas F., 53; William, 53

Handel, CH., 50; Charles H., 59; Frances, 59; Francis, 59; John M., 59; Mary M., 59; Ruth K., 60; William A., 59

Harkcom, Dale W., 67; Violet M., 67; Willard F., 67

Harkins, John W., 5

Harman, Harry E., 63; Jacob, 22; Martha Elizabeth, 18; Susan, 22; Verna F., 63

Harner, Belle W., 44; Edna M. Barclay, 49; Frederick, 44; George E., 44; infant, 43; J. Wilmer, 44; Jesse, 44; John C., 49; Joseph, 43; Marvin, 44, 104; Mary E., 44; Mary K., 45;

Herman, Sarah E., 95

Herr, Abigail, 16; Abram, 12; Alma Mae, 93; Amos, 12; Amos F., 54; Annie, 16; Annie M., 12; Arlean M., 12; B. Frank, 93; Barbara F., 93; Benjamin F., 66; Bertha I., 13; Charles B., 13; Charley, 12; Clara Eva, 12; Clarence S., 12; Clyde R., 10; David H., 10; David Huber, 66; Earlna J., 13; Elizabeth, 12; Elvina, 12; Emma F., 57; Emma Frances, 13; Emma W., 9; Fanny, 10; Fay U., 13; Feuben L., 12; Franklin M., 40; Guy A., 10; Harold E., 67; Harry H., 57; Henry C., 15; Ida E., 13; Isabella, 12, 13; Jacob P., 16; John, 5, 10, 12, 13, 16, 54, 102; John G., 12; John D., 13; John E., 12, 13; John G., 13; Joseph H., 12; Katie M., 12; Laura L., 66; Leah, 10; Lester B., 94; Lettie S., 54; Levi, 10, 14, 102; Lillie L. Barr, 66; Lloyd G., 93; M. Emma, 66; Mabel M., 10, 66; Martha E., 12; Mary, 15; Mary A., 12; Minnie, 94; Myrtle, 54; Paul L., 10; Rebecca, 40; Sarah Jane, 16; Sheriden F., 9; Susan M. Aston, 11; Verna M., 67; Walter R., 66

Hershey, Enos B., 39; Mary, 39

Hershock, Benny Maris, 49

Hess, ---, 5; Alice, 8; Alma Leahman, 68; Amos, 68; Barbie M., 8; Benjamin H., 69; Bertha M., 6; Blaine, 8; Clara G., 8; Daniel, 6, 8; Earl, 8; Edward L., 93; Elila, 69; Eliza, 6; Elsie M., 93; Esta, 8; Esther Martin, 68; George E., 96; H. Franklin, 8; Henry A., 18; Jay Barry, 75; John B., 69; John G., 93; John W., 69; Joyce Weaver, 69; Larry E., 4; Laura Bowers, 96; Louisa, 8; Maris K., 8; Martha, 4; Martha A., 93; Nellie M., 8; Oliva, 8; Ora, 8; Robert, 8; Ruth, 8; Verna N., 75; Warren I., 75

Hickey, Leo, 102

Hieronymus, Rebecca; Fares, 62

Hill, Andrew, 92; Ann, 3, 92; Anna M., 92; Catharine, 92; Enos, 72; Frederick, 92; Goldie Heiney, 72; Helen V., 96; Joseph H., 96; Lizzie, 70; Lizzie M., 70; Mary, 92; Nancy, 92; Susan, 92; William, 70

Himes, William, 32, 102

Hiney, David, 19

Holbein, Emma, 56

Holshouse, Peter, 82, 104

Holtzinger, Amos H., 40; Mary J. Armstrong, 40

Hoopes, Coleman, 25; Eliza J. Gainer, 30; Elizabeth, 30; Harriet, 30; Henry, 30; Jacob Thomas, 30; Maria, 30; Maris, 30; Maris H., 30; Mary Ann, 30; Mary McGreary, 28; William, 30

Hoover, Elmer B., 76; L. Romaine Kurtz, 76

Houpt, Levi R., 92; Margaretta, 93

Huber, Abraham, 23; Anna, 15, 23; Charles S., 13; Doris F., 13; Elinda, 22; Eliza, 15; Elmer, 12; Esther M., 12; Fred, 23;

Kerr, Elizabeth; Brubaker, 27
Kilburn, Blanche O., 60; Charles
    M., 82; Lenard, 105; Lenard C.,
    10; Ruth M., 82
Kilby, Della T., 68; Louis J., 68
Kilmer, Rexford P., 5
Kinsey, Almira E., 54; Annie M.,
    46; Henry H., 54; Shad. B., 54;
    William, 46; William H., 46;
    William K., 46
Kirkwood, Corinea J., 81; Emma
    J., 81; Henry O., 81; Jane, 81;
    R. Fulton, 81; Susan, 81;
    Thomas, 81; Thomas G., 81,
    102
Klein, Annie M., 5; Hans Elias, 5
Kleinhans, Alice S. Helm, 4; Carl
    S., 96, 104; Claude S., 99, 105;
    Cora B. Sickman; Elias L., 4;
    Florence, 96; Fred, 26, 96, 105;
    Frederick L., 99; Harry, 99;
    Lena, 99; Mary, 50; Myrtle, 26;
    Paul, 99; Pearl E., 21; Robert
    M., 99, 105; Roy, 21
Kleinhaus, A., 102
Kleinhuns, U. A., 50
Klump, William W., 86
Kneisley, Emma Lizzie, 16
Kobel, Maria, 80; Martin, 80, 102
Koble, Elias, 74; Elizabeth, 74;
    Jacob, 74; Theressa B., 74;
    William, 74
Koch, Darrell, 100
Kohler, John, 67; Kathryn, 67
Kone, Jesse D., 90
Koplin, Hiram S., 37; Margaret,
    37
Kreider, Amos, 60; B. F., 60;
    Christian, 84; Daniel K., 84;
    Daniel P., 84; David, 86; Elias,
    71; Elizabeth, 84; Elizabeth

Lehman, 19; Flora Bell, 84;
    Franklin, 84; George M., 81; J.
    Calvin, 86; John, 1, 71; John
    M., 84; Lloyd R., 40; M. Fern,
    40; Martha Jane Drumm, 84;
    Martha M., 86; Mary, 71; Mary
    D., 84; Matilda A.; Hessenauer,
    81; Milton S., 86; Samuel H.,
    84; Sarah A., 60; Sophie, 71;
    Unetta, 1
Kreiner, A., 33; E., 33; Victorene
    M., 33
Krider, Charlotte, 13; Jacob, 23;
    Martin, 1; Susan, 23
Krieder, Anna E., 1; Benjamin, 1;
    Calvin, 1; Elizabeth, 1; Francis
    J., 1; John, 1; Martha A., 1
Krow, George W., 32; infant, 32;
    Jane, 32
Krug, Ann, 80; Lucy, 80; Martha
    Ann, 80; Peter, 80; William, 80
Kryder, Barclay, 23; Jacob, 13
Kuhns, John, 59, 102; Sarah C.,
    59
Kunkle, Robert A., 67
Kurtz, Allen Fredrick, 65;
    Amelia, 65; Arthur E., 65;
    Charles A., 65; Christie, 65;
    Emma M., 65; George M., 65;
    Mary A., 65; Mary M. Wiggins,
    65

-L-

Labezius, Elizabeth F. Miller, 56;
    Ella N., 48; Ella Nora, 48;
    George W., 48; Harry, 48;
    Isabella I., 48; Mary A., 48;
    Mary Ann, 48; Myrl S., 48;
    Robert Donald, 56, 105; Russel
    H., 56; Thomas, 48; Thomas J.,
    48; Willie, 48

David, 71; David Howen, 71;
Elizabeth, 62; Margaret, 70;
Philena, 71; Rebecca Mae, 62;
Thomas, 62
Mcalargin, Amos, 22
Mccardel, John, 21; Susanna, 21
Mccardle, Albert, 92; Anna, 47;
Cathrine Christina, 17; Eli, 47;
Joseph, 95; Mary, 95; Rachel,
17; Samuel, 47, 102; Susan, 95;
Washington, 17
Mccauley, Harry B., 64; Jasper
W., 64, 104; Margaret W., 64
Mcclune, Curlus, 61; Emma E.
Frymoyer, 11; Florella, 61;
Harold E., 8; I. Paul, 104; Jean
Joyce, 8; Lindey, 102; Lindley
R., 45; Mabel M., 8; Maris H.,
61; Paul D., 11; Philena Ewing,
45; Rawlins, 96; Susan, 96
Mccombs, Amos, 87, 102; Harry,
36, 102; John, 36; Rebecca, 36;
Thomas, 87, 102
Mccrabb, Abraham, 7; Frank, 6;
Freddie, 6, 7; Jacob, 6; Lizzie,
6, 7
Mccue, James, 35, 103; Nancy, 35
McDonnell, Susanna, 32
McElhaney, Charlota A., 8; D. S.,
8; David S., 5; Sarah A., 8; W.
E., 8
Mceli-ney, 35
McF., H., 77
McFalls, ---, 84; Aldus, 73, 74;
Aldus E., 74; Aldus W., 73;
Chester F., 74; Cora, 73; Della
M., 77; Elizabeth, 73; Emma E.,
74; Esther, 83; Eva C., 73; H.,
85; Harriet, 85; Henry, 77, 83;
Jacob, 83; John, 75, 83; John
C., 85; John W., 77; Margaret,

77, 87; Mary, 77; Oren, 77;
Patrick, 83; Rachel, 77; Rella
E., 73; Ruth B., 75; Sarah, 77;
Sarah Clark, 76; Sue, 75;
Susan, 73; Walter W., 73;
William, 72, 76, 77, 85; William
A., 73; William E., 73; William
H., 73; William W., 73
Mcg., W., 28; William, 28
Mcgaw, James W., 4; Minnie B.,
4; Richard C., 4
Mcgraw, Albert L., 20; Caroline,
20
Mcgreary, Annie Hoopes McC.,
28; Elizabeth, 28; Emma, 28;
James A., 28; James M., 28;
John, 28; M. E., 28; Margaret,
28; Rebecca, 28; Walter S., 28;
William, 28
McKinley, Daisy Minnick, 68;
Robert C., 67
McKinney, Virgie A.; Harner, 44
McL, J., 54
Mclaughlin, Jane, 50; Jennet, 49;
John, 49; Margaret, 49;
Margaret A.; Hambleton, 50;
Mary S., 50; William, 50
McLong, Joseph E., 26
McLune, A. Myrtle, 57; I. Paul,
57
McMcues, Cornelius, 31; Machael,
31; Sarah, 31
McMellen, John, 94; Martha J.
A., 94
McMillan, Gertrude May, 33;
Harry, 33; Harry K., 33;
Isabella, 33; Lurella, 33; Mary
Rebecca, 33
McMillen, Emma, 33; Joseph A.,
33
McNeal, John, 88, 103

58

Moore, Carrie W., 60; Daniel M., 75; Florance R., 44; George Kendig, 31; Hartman, 104; Hartman H., 44; John T., 60; M. M., 60; Mary, 60; Rose A., 75; Ruth, 31; Samuel, 31, 43, 60, 103; Sylvia, 43

Morrison, Ella M., 60; Emma F. Hill, 34; Flora M., 97; Frank, 95, 104; Glenn R., 97; Grace, 34, 95; infants, 34; Joseph E., 34; Kenneth G., 97; Matthew, 34; W. Howard, 34

Morton, Anna, 7; Benjamin, 6, 103; Benjamin F., 7; Delia W., 6; Harrison, 7; Samuel, 7

Moss, Annie S., 39; Emma Evalene, 63; Felix, 31; Frances E., 63; Harriet, 31; J. Frank, 63; James, 31; James H., 39; John, 31; Patrick, 30; Sarah J., 30; Susan, 87; Unity, 31

Mowrer, Elizabeth, 86; Emma Dora, 86; Isaac, 86; Maggie, 86; Tobias, 86

Mueller, Catherine C., 60; G. Michael, 59; L. Christine Spahr, 59; Lestie A., 67; Michael J., 67; Rosa L., 60

Mundorf, Bertha L., 4; Howard M., 4; Pauline, 52; Sarah E., 52; William B., 52

Mundorff, Elizabeth, 63; Elizabeth Herr, 63; Franklin, 63; G. Franklin, 63; George F., 63; Minnie E., 63

Murphy, Marjorie E., 63

Murry, Amos D., 38; Amos E., 37; Carrie E. Brown, 38; Charles E., 38; Daisy E. Shenk, 38;

Erma, 38; Esther I., 37; George, 38; George E., 38; John E., 38; Lester D., 38; Mary L., 38; Minnie E., 38; Myrtle E., 38

Musselman, Effie S., 86; Harry C., 86; John F., 83; Laura A., 83

Musser, Ernest E., 90; Ethel Sellers, 90

Myers, Alice E., 82; Amos C., 82; Anna Adams, 46; Annie Gray, 95; Arlene D., 14; Benjamin, 82; Benjamin F., 82; Essie, 82; Eugene E., 14; George W., 4; Harold B., 14; Harry F., 82; Helen P. Moss, 46; Ida M., 4; Jacob, 82, 104; John G., 90; Lydia E. Miller, 14; M. Jane, 44; Martha, 4; Matthias, 4, 5; Mattias, 4; Meril E., 14; Ruth L., 14; Susan D., 4; Verna M., 14; William B., 46; William Benjamin, 46

Myers-Clark, Bessie G., 43; Joseph H., 43; Mary A., 43; Samuel J., 43

Mylin, G. Gertrude, 86; Holmes R., 87; JoAnn M., 87; S. Miller, 86

-N-

Nagle, Emma M., 81; George, 81

Nau, Charles Henry, 68; Florence, 68

Neel, Audley A., 38; Catherine, 27; Custis D., 36; Emma L., 38; Estella J., 36; Ida S., 36; Jacob M., 36; James, 28; James W., 28; Mary Helen, 38; Rebecca, 28; Thomas, 27; Thomas I., 28;

Rebecca, 99; William, 96

Reinhart, A. Cletus, 70; Ada E., 70; Almon F., 70; Dennis A., 88; Frederick B., 88; Lydia A., 71; Maris M. R., 71; Mary C., 88; Michael R., 70; Rebecca, 71

Renkin, Elaine Hogarth, 24; G. Louise, 1, 4, 32, 42, 57, 68, 69; Louisa, 24; William M., 24

Rennel, Sarah, 3

Resch, Edward L., 18; Lou Marie Rhinier, 18

Ressel, Abbie J., 9; Blanche E., 10; Charles, 6; Clara M., 6; Edith Elva, 10; Eva E. Gainer, 10; Frank G., 9; George W., 92; Maris B., 10; Martha N. Trissler, 6; Murvan C., 6

Ressler, Barbara, 90; Carrie R. Cramer, 42; Clarence E., 42; Ephraim, 90; Leigh M., 76; Minnie Fisher, 76

Rhinier, Bertha C., 10; Daniel S., 18; Edith R., 18; Edna M., 18; Harvey, 10; Harvey H., 18; Lou Marie Resch, 18; Susan J., 10

Rhoades, Mabel E., 66; Samuel F., 66; Viola M., 60

Rhoads, Charles F., 73; Jacob, 59, 103; Mary C., 59; Virginia Brubaker, 27

Rice, Barbara Warfel, 94; E. Fred, 37; Franklin, 94; Frederick, 90, 92, 103; Henry, 37; Jane, 75; John, 37, 75, 103; John B., 29; Louisa C. Campbell, 90; Maris, 37, 90; Martha, 92; Mary, 75; Mary J., 37; Peter, 35; William, 92

Richmond, Arlean, 100; Harry, 100

Rineer, A., 9; Aaron, 8, 91; Catherine M., 94; Edward F., 91; Eliza Ann, 9; Emma, 84, 92; Emma F., 9; Fred K., 77; Harriet, 75; Harriet E., 75; Harrison H., 75; Hattie M., 77; Jesse, 94, 104; Job E., 9; John, 84; M., 9; Margaret, 9; Martin, 75; Martin E., 75; Rebecca, 91; Retta M., 91; Susan B., 9

Rinier, Benjamin E., 90; Bertha C., 94; Charles A., 99; J. W., 98; J. Westley, 98; John M., 94; Joseph G., 98, 103; Joseph H., 90; Martin V., 94; Mary Alice, 94; Matilda E., 98; Mildred M., 98; Reba V., 94; Ruth May, 99

Ritchie, Edward E., 75; Frances A., 75; James M., 75; James W., 75; Minnie N., 75

Ritter, Mary Ethel C., 74; Paul R., 74

Roach, Mary T., 79

Robinson, F. T., 61; Isaac, 43; Rachel, 43

Rohrer, Flora E., 80; Jay, 79; Jay M., 80

Rombach, Linda A. Myers, 14; Robert E., 14

Root, Terry L., 67

Ross, infant dau., 12; Irene May, 12; M. A., 12; Mary A., 12; W. W., 12; William W., 12

Rosser, Andrew P., 73; Myrtle, 73; Phyllis A. West, 73

Rosso, Esther A. Cully, 11

Ruher, Amos, 85; Frankie, 85; Martha, 85

Rutter, Annie Alice Harner, 44; Harry B., 43

-S-

Saber, May L., 99; Virginia, 99; William, 99

Sanders, Emma Miller, 76

Sangrey, Ira D., 81

Savery, Ann, 2; Edward, 2; George S., 2; William T., 2

Schaffer, Johannes, 20

Schenck, Barbara, 22; Christian, 22

Schenckin, Anna, 22

Schenokin, Barbara, 22

Schmeltz, Jacob, 21

Schmidt, Emma A., 26; Henrich, 21; Jacob, 21; Jacob J., 26; John M., 26; Magadalena, 21; Suie E., 26

Schmith, Johannes, 21

Schweicker, Christinna Schwenk, 20; Felix, 20; Sebastian, 20; Sebr., 101

Seabrooks, Agnes, 20; Esther, 20; James, 20; Jesse, 20; William, 20

Seiple, Bessie N., 53; E. L., 46; Elizabeth E., 46; Ida M., 46; John L., 46; Joseph, 46; L. R., 46; Lindley R., 46; Luella R., 53; M. A., 53; Mary A., 53; Paul I., 46; Verna M., 53; W. H., 53; William H., 53

Sellers, Annie E., 90; Chester M., 38; Cornelia, 95; Daisy, 94; Edward J., 90; Frank, 39; George D., 90; Harry H., 95; Hazel B., 50; infant, 50; James, 50; John W., 94; Laraine, 98; Martha, 90; Martha J., 90; Richard W., 98; Viola M., 39, 95; William, 39, 90, 95, 103; William H., 90

Senft, Annie S., 92; Edward, 92; Fannie Z., 92; Howard, 92; Mary, 92; Sarah, 92; Solomon, 92

Sensenig, Annie L., 79; John D., 5; John K., 79

Shank, Alf, 15, 16; Alfred, 16; Clara E., 16; David, 21, 103; Edwin Levi, 9; Elizabeth, 15, 16; Fanny, 21; Hiram, 78; Irwin H., 16; Jacob, 21; Martin H., 16; Mary, 78; Sallie E., 15

Shaub, Arthur Z., 43; Benjamin C., 49, 105; Clara Cramer, 43; Clarence A., 49; infant, 49; Mae Elizabeth, 49; Marian S., 49; Ross Aldus, 48; Ruth E., 43

Shaubach, James, 105; James S., 67, 105; Kathryn Nordsick, 67

Shenck, Catharine, 93; Elias, 93; Henry S., 93; Jonas, 93; Judith, 93; Levi, 92; Margaret, 92; Mary, 93; Mary Wesley, 93; Rudalph, 93

Shenk, Amoss M., 37; Ann, 37; Anna, 93; Annie E. Sellers, 37; Carrie, 77; Christian, 93; Edna, 26; Elizabeth A., 60; Emma N. Rineer, 77; Harry C., 77; Helen K., 57; Henry, 93; J. Andrew, 26; John, 77; Lee M., 57; Lottie, 77; Martin G., 37

Shertzer, John W., 93; Mary H., 99; Ray L., 99, 104; Robert L., 99

Shickley, Eli, 24; Sarah J., 24

Shiffer, D. Pearl Lefever, 66; Harriet E., 66; John, 104; John E., 66, 104

Shingler, Howard F., 86

Shirk, Amos, 64, 80; Martha A.,

Warren, 23; Wilmer G., 50

Snavely, Ellen J., 46; Henry, 76; John, 46; Martha, 76

Snodgrass, Margaret, 47

Snyder, Adam, 88; Della C., 84; Henry, 88; Sarah J., 8

Sowers, Amanda C., 39; Conrad, 39, 103

Spangler, baby girl, 11

Spence, Barbara, 73; Gabriel, 5, 73, 78; Jesse, 36; John, 78; John B., 73; Lodowick, 73; Martha, 78; Mary, 78; Rebecca, 36; Ulich, 73

Stack, Catherine, 18; Elizabeth, 18; Henry Clay, 18; Mary, 18

Stamm, David P., 99; Elizabeth R. Titzel, 99

Stansbury, Sue F., 60; Warren, 60; William S., 60

Stauffer, Abraham W., 19; Annie E., 73; Barbara, 22; Christian, 22; Elizabeth, 54; Fannie M., 43; Frank, 57; H. Clayton, 73; Henry, 54; Hiram, 43; Jacob, 22; Johanne, 22; Lelia K., 49; Margaret, 22; Maria, 19; Ralph E., 49; Samuel, 57

Steiner, Benjamin F., 10; Harry, 10; Mabel, 10

Stephens, T. M., 56, 103

Stevenson, Dorothy E., 41; Emma E. Shoff, 39; George E., 39; Joan P., 57; Martha E., 49; Mary, 39; Nancy E., 49; S. C., 39, 103; Samuel E., 41; William E., 57; William F., 49

Steveson, Elizabeth, 2; Elizabeth Jane, 2; John, 2

Stewart, Alirad, 28; Gora A., 28; Margaret, 28; Thomas, 28;

Willie, 28

Stively, Frank, 50; Lewis, 50; Mary, 42; Myrtle, 50; Myrtle S., 50; Thomas, 42

Stokes, Charles, 67; Dan, 61; Daniel, 61; Elsie B., 67; Harry D., 61; Ida Duffy, 59; Jacob R., 39; Rettie, 61; Sarah R. Sellers, 61; Suie J., 39; Willis Earl, 59

Stoner, Christian, 18

Stotzman, Joseph, 69

Stouter, Anna, 18

Stripe, Nellie F., 4

Sullivan, Eliza A., 60; James A., 60; Katie E., 60

Sweicker, Agnes Marie, 20

Sweigart, Benjamin L., 42; Cathrine, 19; Ed, 21; Edmund, 21; Edward M., 19; Elmer E., 84; Felix, 19, 84, 101; Felix C., 42; Felix W., 19; George F., 84; George Leroy, 27; George W., 19; Jacob, 19; John, 19, 42; Katie L., 27; M. Elizabeth Clark, 42; Martha, 19; Martha M., 19; Mary, 19, 21; Mary A., 42; Sarah A., 84; Theresa M., 42; William, 27

Sweigert, Henry, 21

Swigart, Catherine, 16; Felix, 16

-T-

Tangert, Mary E. Beach, 7

Taylor, Julianna, 95; Martha, 95; William J., 95

Terrell, George W., 11; Grace M., 11

Thomas, Albert, 85, 103; Barbara, 17; Cathrine, 17; Ella E., 68; John, 17; Sandy, 69; Sandy P., 68; Sarah J., 85

Thompson, Harry, 56; Hiram L.,
71, 103; Tilghman, 71
Tominson, Emanuel F., 63;
Maggie A., 63; Ross E., 63;
Ruth E., 63
Tomlinson, A. Jane, 35; Amanda
L., 45; Blanche, 74; Edgar M.,
40; Ella D., 40; John J., 45;
Rickey W., 35; Willard, 35;
William R., 74
Trafford, Mary F., 96
Transue, Edwin Allen, 46; Grace
Kauffman, 46
Trimble, Addison J., 66; Anna
Gamber, 66; Eliza, 42; James
H., 42; Harriet M., 65; Mary B.,
65; Olive M., 66; Ruth Cramer,
52; Thomas J., 65, 103; W.
Lester, 52; William, 66; William
R., 65
Trissler, Benjamin F., 79; David
T., 58; Mabel M., 58; Orello V.,
79; Sarah, 58
Trout, Donald, 15; Geneva, 15;
George M., 15
Turner, Albert L., 16; Ernest S.,
90; Ethel L., 16

-U-

Uffelmann, ---, 95; Anna Mary
Charlotte Spardbden, 95
Uffleman, William, 31, 103
Unsworth, Edna M., 97
Urban, Benjamin F., 81, 103;
Cecilia H., 9; Clyde E., 9;
Dorothy M., 57; Edna Douglas,
57; Edna K., 57; Emma L., 13;
Guy K., 57; Jeanne M., 9;
Jennie M., 13; Joseph W., 13;
W. Victor, 57

-V-

Vandyke, Elizabeth, 2; Joseph, 2
Villee, Ada Moss, 63; Edgar R.,
63
Vollrath, John A., 86; Maria S.,
86

-W-

Wade, Grace V., 19
Wagner, Clarence C., 95;
Elizabeth, 94; Elizabeth E., 99;
Frederick, 95; George, 94;
Helen L., 98; infant, 94; Jesse
E., 99; Kathryn, 97; Laura E.,
95; Lawrence, 98; Mary A., 90;
Mary H., 96; Mary M., 98;
Peter, 90, 103; Richard C., 97,
105; Richard E., 97; Thomas
Bruce, 97; William F., 96
Wallace, Benjamin J., 38; Elenora
E., 2; Mary A., 2; Martha, 2;
Minnie E., 38; Nancy, 2; Sarah,
2; William, 2
Waller, Kenneth Charles; J., 41
Walter, Adeline J., 90; Catharine,
17; Frank W., 90; George, 90;
Jacob, 17, 90
Walton, Amos, 28, 52; Anna
Margie, 28; Annetta C., 32;
Annie, 59; Annie E., 59;
Barbara Ellen, 32; Bertha D.,
59; Earl, 66; Edward L., 40;
Elizabeth, 32; Elmer A., 55;
Hannah, 28; Harriet J.
Appleton, 55; Isaac, 28; Jesse,
32; John M., 59; Joseph, 32;
Louella A., 55; M. Della, 59;
Mahlon, 59; Mahlon Y., 59;
Mary J., 40; William A., 59
Warfel, Abraham W., 19; Albert
D., 100; Alice, 99; Amos R., 37;

Amos S., 93; Andrew, 99; Anna,
80; Annie, 95; Barbara, 19;
Carrie I., 87; Catharine, 93;
Cora M., 100; Daniel, 23; David,
6; Earnest R., 80; Elias, 4;
Elizabeth, 4, 23; Fredy D., 95;
George, 19; Gladys N., 100;
Gregory Scott, 67; H. Gary, 67;
Henry, 23; Henry H., 80; Ida
M. Sellers, 37; Levi W., 95;
Mabel, 37; Magdalena, 23;
Margaret S., 6; Marion G., 100,
105; Myrtle, 80, 100; Sarah, 78;
Shirley, 67; William, 78;
William R., 100
Warpenstein, Charles H., 24;
Jacob Shickley, 24; Susan A.,
24
Warren, Amelia H., 6; J.
Raymond, 6; Paul Lee, 6;
William W., 6
Weaver, Berl W., 100; Grace N.,
87; John Mark, 15; Pearl E.,
100; R. Morris, 87; Rhoda E.,
15; Robert W., 100
Weidler, Aaron G., 99; Gordon,
99; Hilda, 99; Phillip Gordon,
99
Weidlich, Anna M., 6; Catharine,
15; David L., 6; Ernest M., 15,
103; Godfreid, 69; infant, 69; J.
W. W., 69; Susanna, 69
Weitzel, Anna Eshleman, 67;
Charles E., 92; Fannie P., 92;
Paul W., 67
Welk, Joan, 100; Kenneth, 100;
Lisa M., 100
Wells, Amemia, 54; Clare
Ballantyne, 56; Ward E., 54, 56
Wentz, Charles Elvin, 45; E. Roy,
45; Hariet P., 49; John S., 46;

Joseph, 46; Leila E. Eshleman,
45; Louisa A., 45; Marinda H.,
49; Mary J., 49; Paul, 45;
Sarah, 46; Sarah A. Penny, 46;
Susan, 46; Thomas, 49; Viola
Webster, 46; Violetta, 49;
Walter G., 45; William H., 45;
Winfield S., 49
Wenzel, Barbara, 13; Fred, 13;
Jean, 13
Whirlow, Harry, 5
White, Charles, 54; Henry, 92;
James, 48, 103; Margaret A.,
48; Mary, 92
Whitmyer, Charles Westley, 100;
Nettie A., 100
Wiederrecht, Lloyd G., 20, 104;
Maria C., 20
Wiggins, Clair T., 67; Clayton, 80,
103; Edna Carpenter, 9; Frank
M., 43; Harriet, 80; Leroy S.,
80; Lillie E., 43; May A. Funk,
67; Mazie M. Evena, 80; Ross,
105; Ross W., 9; William C., 80
Wilhelm, Jacob, 93
Wilson, Barbara, 78; Benjamin,
78; Catharine, 78; Catharine E.,
69; Elizabeth H., 79; James, 78;
Jane, 69, 78; John, 69, 78; John
M., 69; Josh, 60; Josiah, 79;
Josiah Jeffers, 60; Mary, 4;
Mathias, 4; Matthias, 4; Rachel,
60
Winters, A. Lewis, 62; C.
Columbus, 73; Edward M., 61;
Elizabeth, 61; Ella M., 62;
George, 61; Harry C., 33; I.
Clayre, 61, 105; M. Myrtle, 9;
Washington C., 9
Wirth, Aaron, 73; Abbigail, 73;
Abigail, 73; Paul, 73; Serenus,

73

Wise, Frederick, 96

Wissler, Anna Mary Bowers, 96;
Charles D., 67; Chester E., 41;
Daniel Herr, 85; Edna M. Null,
67; John R., 96; Robert A., 67;
Sylvia Heiney, 85

Witmer, Arthur, 59

Wood, Esther, 68; Robert W., 68

Worfel, Daniel H., 4; Susan B., 4

-Y-

Yenner, Conrad, 15

Yingling, E., 20; Emanuel, 20;
Emma, 20; Esther A., 20; G.;
George, 20, 103; Lydia Ann, 20;
Mary Jane, 20

Yost, Clayton, 9; Emma, 44;
Emma P., 44; Harry Y., 10;
Henry, 9; Irma Clare, 44; John
R., 44; Rebecca, 9; Rena C., 10;
Samuel, 9

Young, Barbara A., 20; Carl, 19;
Henry, 20; Ioua E. Boatman,
19; John C., 19; Mandi H., 19;
Samuel, 20; Thomas B., 19;
Violet, 10; Virgie B., 10;
William, 10

-Z-

Zappulla, Benjamin, 34; Samuel,
34

Zehman, Edmund, 20

Zercher, Andrew J., 19; Betty
Mae, 9; Helen M., 19

www.ingramcontent.com/pod-product-compliance
Lightning Source LLC
Chambersburg PA
CBHW071807090426
42737CB00012B/1982